STREET SMART

SUCCEEDING IN A MAN'S WORLD

Dina LaPolt

MEDIA

BURMAN BOOKS
MEDIA CORP.

BURMAN BOOKS
MEDIA CORP.
MEDIA

Published 2025 by Gildan Media LLC, aka G&D Media
by arrangement with Burman Books Media Corp.
www.GandDmedia.com

Edited by Lara Petersen
Front and back cover photos by Bonnie Schiffman
Book Design by Clarissa D'Costa

Library of Congress Cataloging-in-Publication Data is
available upon request

ISBN: 978-1-7225-9910-2

10 9 8 7 6 5 4 3 2 1

STREET
SMART

To my amazing boys, Wilson Ray and Buddy Lee.
This book is for you.

As you both grow and learn, I hope you recognize how fortunate you are to be raised by strong, resilient women—not just your moms, Mama Dina and Mommy Wendy, but also your grandmothers, Grandma Donna and Grandma Susan ("V V") who never took shit from anybody; your aunties, Corinne, Mel, and Sarah; and Angela Haro, a staple in our lives.

Being raised by strong women means you've witnessed what it takes to stand up for your beliefs, face challenges head-on, and—most importantly—show compassion to others. I hope you carry the lessons with you always. Use the strength and wisdom you've inherited to make a positive impact in the world. Embrace the values of resilience, empathy, and integrity in everything you do.

Remember, the strength you see in the women who raised you is rooted not just in power, but in love, kindness, humility, and your personal commitment to help other people. Always stand up for the underdog. You have a legacy of strength behind you—let it inspire you to become the best version of yourselves and honor all the incredible women who have guided you and will continue to be the guiding lights in your lives.

People will forget what you said,
people will forget what you did,
but people will never forget
how you made them feel.
—**MAYA ANGELOU**

Contents

1

Overcoming Predispositioned Obstacles

I am a power bitch. At least that's what they call me. I have my own entertainment law firm in Los Angeles, which is the only one of its stature owned and operated by a sole female attorney. We represent some of the biggest names in music and we also represent talent in film, television, and fashion. My office is in the historic 9000 Sunset Boulevard building on the world-renowned Sunset Strip in West Hollywood. It's directly across the street from the world-famous Rainbow Bar & Grill and The Roxy Theatre, where legendary artists such as Bruce Springsteen, Chuck Berry, Tina Turner, Smokey Robinson, Stevie Wonder, Aretha Franklin, Mötley Crüe, and many others have played. The 9000 Sunset building is where Jim Morrison from The Doors perched himself on the roof, thinking he was a bird after taking LSD, as memorialized in his biography, *No One Here Gets Out Alive*. I have my dream job and my life is amazing. But it wasn't always this way.

I had a terrible drug and alcohol addiction. I'm also gay and grew up during a time when it wasn't cool to be gay. In fact, in certain pockets of America, cohabiting in a same-sex romantic relationship was against the law. I had to overcome a lot of obstacles to get where I am now, and *none* of it was easy. Several times I flat-out *failed*. I had to stop seeking people's approval or validation, especially when their opinions about what I should do with my life held me back.

I grew up in a patriarchal family system in New Paltz, which is ninety miles north of New York City. My dad was the so-called "breadwinner," and my mom was responsible for raising me, my brother and sister, and taking care of the family. My brother, Glenn, is three years younger than me, and my sister, Corinne, is two years younger than Glenn. New Paltz was formed in the eighteenth century by the French Huguenots, who left Europe to escape religious persecution. That set the tone for the town. Black people migrated there during slavery so they could live as free people. One of the most celebrated Black people who lived in New Paltz was Sojourner Truth, an American abolitionist and activist for African American civil rights and women's rights. Since she lived there in the mid-nineteenth century, the whole town has found ways to honor her name. There's the Sojourner Truth Peace Park, the Sojourner Truth Library at the college, and a monument to commemorate her as well as a dedication at the Walkway Over the Hudson, which crosses over the Hudson River from Highland to Poughkeepsie. It's awesome!

My parents grew up even farther upstate in what's commonly referred to as the Borscht Belt, where a lot of Jewish people migrated after the Holocaust. Ironically, both my father and mother are Catholic. My mother's side of the family was very conservative, and Dad's side was made up of alcoholics. My paternal grandfather fixed school buses for a living and his wife drank from the minute she woke up to the minute she went to bed. They owned a bungalow colony in Woodbourne, New York, a place where Jewish people from New York City would spend their summers, arriving in May and leaving when the colony closed on Labor Day. As the years went on, I learned that many of my dad's cousins died of alcoholism. My mother's family lived in Loch Sheldrake, New York, and owned a huge family home that would house the overflow of people from the Shady Nook, a small resort hotel nearby. With all these Jewish families surrounding them, they learned how to make Jewish food for their guests, even though my grandparents were derivative Catholics who were basically racist and homophobic.

They called my mother the Black Sheep of the family. She was the oldest daughter of five kids. Although she went to a community college and majored in home economics, she was her own person. A very strong woman. After graduating, she moved to New York City, against her parents' wishes. She dated my dad before moving, and even after she broke up with him, he would still drive down to the city and sit at the counter where she was waiting tables. My mother didn't pay him any mind, but eventually he won her over and they married.

My maternal grandparents wanted to bequeath some property from the Loch Sheldrake family home to my father, which was more of a ploy to control him and keep their daughter near the family home. They didn't like my dad because he was kind of wild, a womanizer, and a drinker. At the time, he was a prison guard, but went back to school to get his college degree. After getting two master's degrees, he spent most of his forty-year career with the New York State prison system at Green Haven, a maximum-security prison, where he was involved with prison reform. After noticing that most prisoners were Black, while the majority of prison employees were white, he set out to change that by setting up educational programs for prisoners. These prisoners wouldn't keep getting sent back to prison if they were educated and had some hope for their future.

My mother took on a significant role within the community by becoming a community leader, co-founding the New Paltz Youth Center in the 1980s, and starting the Gay and Lesbian Alliance. She helped raise money when the New York Panther 21 members were arrested in 1969 and charged with over 150 felony counts.

One of the members of New York Panther 21s was Afeni Shakur, Tupac's mother. During the height of the Black Panther movement, she wrote for the Black Panther newspaper and was a section leader of the Harlem chapter of the Black Panther Party. When they were all arrested, a lot of the progressives were livid because they knew it was just the government trying to hold Black people down.

When the judge set bail for the Black Panthers, they all agreed Afeni should get out first because she was a great public speaker. She could raise money for the others to secure bail. In her biography, she talks about the "well-meaning white women" from the church who helped raise funds. She told me some of them were from upstate New York. One of them was my mother. So, growing up, I knew all about Afeni Shakur and the Black Panther Party.

Looking at my family history, my paternal grand-parents' drunkenness affected my father, which created my predisposition to alcoholism and struggles with addictions. My maternal grandparents were very conservative and had old-fashioned ideas and expectations that they wanted to impose on my mother. She rebelled against them and went to New York City to do her own thing. It's through her that I got my drive.

My home was subject to patriarchal control, which was common during that era. My dad was in charge of everything and made all the money. That's just how things were in the town I grew up in. The men were in charge. Everybody with authority was male. The mayor, the police chief, the fire chief, the school principals, and so on. The townspeople revolved around the Catholic church, and all the priests were male. Male dominance is what I saw all around me. Because of the traditional patriarchal system, a lot of women grow up waiting for "permission" or validation from the men in their lives, whether conscious or subconscious. In such an environment, I was under a heavy influence to be no different from the rest of the women.

New Paltz is home to a prominent liberal arts college: The State University of New York (a.k.a. SUNY New Paltz). Even though the town proper is conservative, New Paltz is forty minutes outside of Woodstock,

New York. It's a hippie town, as far as the college is concerned. Many of my teachers in high school kept their long hair in ponytails and wore Birkenstocks. So, in contrast, there was the college town, which was progressive and liberal, and then there was the town proper run by mostly Irish Catholic men who were somewhat conservative.

Given the town's prevailing culture at the time, I had a predisposition to be more submissive—to believe men did the leading. School had classes like home economics, which taught girls the role of being a homemaker and how to be the best possible house-wife, or to become nurses or teachers. None of it was right for me, but I didn't know how to advocate for myself. At age five, I started taking guitar lessons, and I loved it! I loved music. I wanted to become a musi-cian. My father felt I should learn something else so I'd have something to fall back on. He always implied I was going to fail. He didn't think I could have a future as a musician.

It was my mother who advocated for me and showed me I didn't have to conform. Although she was heavily involved with the church, she didn't buy into any of its bullshit. She believed in women's rights. I saw my mother going against the grain. She always gravitated toward people of color. An African fam-ily moved into the trailer park up the road from us.

One of the girls, Bernadine, became one of my best friends. My mother related more to outsiders, as she felt like an outsider herself. She used to tell people, "I always knew where to find my daughter on the playground. I would just look for the Black kids."

In my town at that time, being gay was highly stigmatized. In the summer, we'd all go to Moriello Pool where the townspeople would always talk about "those lesbians from the college." According to a community full of white, Irish Catholics, lesbians were overweight, hairy women. I knew I was gay when I was in kindergarten, and I was acutely aware of how everyone had their own ideas of who fit or didn't fit a particular label. The assumption was that people should be straight, not gay, but I knew I liked girls in a different way.

When I was in kindergarten, I had the biggest crush on this girl named Nancy. Of course, I couldn't tell people I was gay. I vividly remember going to church every Sunday and seeing a newsletter that prohibited churchgoers from listening to "hell songs." One of them was Eric Clapton's "Layla." This astonished me because I had just asked my guitar teacher, John Anderson, to teach it to me. He was also our middle school music teacher. The church dictated who we should be under the guise of saving us from evil and ourselves. To this day, I have no idea what they had against Eric Clapton.

I was very lucky to have my mother. She led by example and showed me to fight what my father, society, and the era had preordained for a female. With her there to guide me, my battles weren't as hard as they had been for countless other women. The things young girls are taught become deeply rooted in who they become. Imposed ideals can become obstacles to becoming who you were meant to be, but you can overcome them. It starts with reprogramming your mind. Connect with that internal young girl again and listen to what she says. The more you do that, the better prepared you will be to break free of the restraints imposed on you by others.

When I was in high school, there was a guidance counselor who we all really loved, but he got fired one day, right out of the blue! I marched down to the administration office to find out what had happened, but they wouldn't give an explanation. They basically said, "Go back to class. It's none of your business . . . Adult stuff." I went home. I got off the bus. I cried my eyes out. Clear as day, I can still hear my mother saying, "Well, what are you going to do about it?" I looked at her, dumbfounded. "This is unacceptable. So, literally, what are you going to do about it?"

That night, she and I sat there making a protest flyer. She drove me to make copies and then to school the next day. I had the whole thing planned: a student walkout and a protest to oppose firing the guidance counselor. The school district superintendent called my mom and told her to please get the students back into school. She scoffed and said, "Why are you calling me? Dina's in charge. Go talk to her." With that, she hung up the phone. So, the superintendent proceeded to negotiate with me using letters (which I still have). He was negotiating with *me*! I said I would get the students back into the school with an understanding that the district would rehire the guidance counselor. And they did.

You cannot change your family structure or the circumstances you were born into, nor can you change where you were born or where you were raised. These factors shape your way of being and seeing the world, which may not always be beneficial or an accurate reflection of who you are. It's what you knew—what you were exposed to and what examples you had to learn from, directly or subconsciously. Those experiences become ingrained and shape your mind so you become who you think you should be. They influence your psyche so powerfully that many people don't even recognize that it affects their life choices because, often, other people are pushing their opinions and agendas on you without you even soliciting their input.

Seek out other people who will support your ideas, including the people on social media who are doing exactly what you want to do. Don't let others compromise your dreams and desires. People will always try to hold you back because they want you to stay where *they* want you to be for *their* benefit, or to ease *their* fear and anxiety, even if that place isn't where you want to be.

You can do this through various means: school events, conferences, and networking events, and through the internet. Social media has created a huge opportunity for access. Platforms such as LinkedIn, Instagram, and even TikTok open doors to reach out and connect with people. People check their social media accounts (including direct messages) several times throughout the day, even if they've contracted a third-party social media company to run their accounts. *They still have access.* No matter what profession they're in, everyone loves adulation. If you reach out to a power woman you admire and tell her how much you admire her and why, chances are she'll eventually see that message and respond, especially if you reach out a few times.

Be proactive. Reach out. Don't be intimated; however, keep your message brief and to the point. Don't be a stalker. That will only freak her out. Always be a professional. Remember that almost everyone started at the bottom, *especially* women. Don't let your age get in the way. Whether you're twenty-eight or sixty, life is for living. Leave fear at the door.

Think of "FEAR" as False Evidence Appearing Real.

Believe in yourself. It's okay to put yourself first. There's no better time than right now. Look for mentors. The whole world is available to you.

Society can pressure you to limit yourself or to think some things aren't possible, especially when they're related to your age. Young people don't think they're old enough to do something and older people think it's too late to do something. Neither is true. You're never too old or too young to chase your dreams. Only you can say what you can and cannot do, and it's not dictated by your age.

I was twenty-eight years old and in my first year of law school at John F. Kennedy School of Law in Walnut Creek, California, situated in the East Bay outside of San Francisco. One of my study partners was a sixty-two-year-old woman, Elsa Ortiz. Even though Elsa was in law school at night, she worked full time during the day for California State Senator Bill Lockyer. She was in law school because she always wanted to be a lawyer. You are never too old to pursue your dreams.

Mariah Comer, a twenty-five-year-old woman, was in her third year of law school. A first-generation college student of Black and Mexican descent, Mariah grew up in Santa Ana, California, where the school dropout rate was 45 percent and only 12 percent of the population held a bachelor's degree or higher. Mariah was part of that 12 percent when she applied to law school. Dreaming of one day becoming an entertainment attorney representing rap and hip-hop music artists, she attended an entertainment law networking event during her third year of law school. She sought out female lawyers who looked like her and spotted a young Black attorney who was working as a new junior attorney at a talent agency in Los Angeles. She had just passed the 2017 California State bar exam, which is taken over three consecutive days, and is considered one of the hardest, if not *the* hardest, bar exam in the country. Mariah introduced herself and told the young attorney about her own entertainment law aspirations.

The attorney connected Mariah with another Black female attorney, Danielle Price, who was working at a prominent boutique entertainment law firm owned by a sole female attorney—me! I had just put Danielle on the account handling rapper 21 Savage when she brought Mariah in for an interview. Mariah became our intern for the next year and then an attorney at the firm shortly after passing the California State bar exam. We put Mariah on the accounts of some of today's biggest rap music artists, including Cardi B, Tyga, and YG. Mariah made partner at the firm at age twenty-eight. So— you are never too young.

For almost twenty years, I taught the Legal and Practical Aspects of the Music Business class at UCLA. About thirteen years into it, some friends from Soul Cycle and I got involved in the nonprofit organization called Urban Fitness 911. One of those friends was Tatiana Hachett, a high school chemistry teacher at King Drew High School in Compton, one of the Gateway Cities of Los Angeles. It's south of Downtown and mainly known for being the birthplace of famous rappers such as Dr. Dre, N.W.A, and Kendrick Lamar. The goal of Urban Fitness 911 was to educate and improve health and nutrition in low-income communities.

We helped Tatiana bring some students from KDHS to Soul Cycle in West Hollywood for Angela Manuel Davis's 6:00 A.M. spin class. Angela was an Urban Fitness 911 member, celebrity trainer, and motivational speaker. I got to know the KDHS students and realized some of them had a deep passion for music. Tatiana arranged for me to attend the high school to give a presentation on the music business. When I educated the students on over fifty different jobs and careers in the music industry, these kids' faces lit up.

For the next seven years, I worked with Tatiana, the KDHS administration, and UCLA to award ten students each year with a scholarship to attend my UCLA music business class. At the end of each semester, I invited Tatiana and the ten students to my office for a get-together so they could meet some of the young law students and attorneys working for me.

At one of these get-togethers, Tatiana looked around my office at all the platinum and gold plaques my artists had been bestowed upon me over the years. She said, "It's so inspiring that you're living your life's passion and have been able to create such an amazing career. I wish I had met you when I was these kids' age." To which I replied, "Aren't you living your dream because you're so passionate about these students and this school?" She says, "Of course, I love what I do, and I love these kids, but my dream has always been to go to medical school and become a doctor." At that time, she was thirty-four years old. At thirty-eight, she went to medical school. At forty-two, she finished her fourth year clinicals, completed medical school, and is currently a first-year resident doctor. So, it's never too late.

CHAPTER JOURNAL NOTES

- What personal or societal barriers do you need to overcome?
- What preconceived notions do you have about yourself?
- What have people said you could or should be?
- Get in touch with your inner self—the person you rarely reveal to others.
- Spend time identifying who that person is and what characteristics, strengths, and values you possess.
- Find mentors—people who align with the real you. Reach out. Learn from them.
- Refuse to be confined to the boxes you were put into and allow yourself to bloom.

Without apology.

2

Believe in Yourself and
Put Yourself First

When I was in the seventh grade, I couldn't do math. Back then, schools didn't have formal evaluations to diagnose learning disabilities. They simply told my mother I had dyslexia and that, instead of going to the New Paltz High School, I should go to the vocational school. That's where students who wanted to become mechanics, hairdressers, and the like would attend. My mother refused to send me there. She told the school officials I was staying in the New Paltz school district because I loved music and the music teachers. And that I was happy and healthy there. And to do whatever it took to teach me what I needed to learn. Thank God for my mother!

I started a rock band when I was thirteen. Except for my music teacher and mother, I didn't receive much support for doing that. I sought inspiration from the women who were doing what I wanted to do, like Joan Jett and Pat Benatar. Joan Jett was one of my favorite artists growing up. I ended up being her opening act when I was in college, and now I'm her lawyer.

This is why I stress the importance of seeking connections. I resonated with these women who played guitar. I loved Joan Jett, and that's why I started playing the guitar. Not a lot of women did in those days. As I got to know Joan Jett, I learned a lot about her career path. Her story is amazing. She started out with the all-girl band The Runaways. After they broke up, twenty-three labels rejected her demos, which featured songs like "I Love Rock 'n' Roll" and "Bad Reputation," and probably only because she wore leather and played the guitar. Back then, only guys were "supposed to" wear leather and play the guitar the way Joan Jett did.

With Kenny Laguna as her producer and co-songwriter, Joan Jett carved out her own path. Kenny was also her manager, and together they pressed up their own vinyl and sold them at shows from the trunk of Kenny's Cadillac. That's how Blackheart Records was born. Together, they drove all over the East Coast to local radio stations, handing out records and making connections. Fans demanded that radio stations play "I Love Rock 'n' Roll," which is how it became a

No. 1 hit in America. The band members themselves found out it was a hit when they heard it on the radio themselves. Forty years later, Joan and Kenny are still together, touring, making music, and running the world. Kenny's daughter, Carianne, is now running Blackheart Records. Instead of conforming, Joan Jett did things her own way, defying the expectations society placed on women.

Music was a big part of my mother's life. She always had something playing and knew stories about every artist she listened to. She told me how John Denver lived in Colorado on a farm and was learning how to be a pilot, and that people didn't like Karen Carpenter because she played the drums. You know, because only men were "supposed" to play the drums.

My mother also played Billie Holiday. She told me people didn't like Billie either because she was a woman, and she was Black. My mother taught me that Black people were lynched in America, and the people didn't like Billie because she sang about it in one of her songs.

Those at-home lessons about music were little steps toward making sure everything I connected with held importance. Believing in yourself and feeling that strength is important, and you need to hold on to it. What I wanted to do was important and valuable to *me*. I did it regardless of what everybody told me. Regardless of what the school told me. Writing a list of jobs for women on a fucking blackboard in high school is bullshit. Who wants to do any of that?

When I was twenty-four years old and living in New York, I had just graduated from the State of New York College at New Paltz with a bachelor's degree in music. Although I played in a band, I had always wanted to be on the business side of things. I helped run the college concert committee, Jedi Productions, and held a part-time internship as Eric Carr's assistant. At the time, Eric was the drummer for the rock band, KISS.

I was dating a girl named Andrea, and things were quickly becoming serious . . . for *her*. She was from a hot-blooded New York Italian family and was fiercely possessive of me. Her constant need to know where I was and who I was with was relentless. It wasn't long before my patience with Andrea had grown so thin that I needed an escape when KISS and their business team decided to move to California. Eric sold his New York apartment and moved to Los Angeles. And just like that, I decided I was moving to California, too. I had no idea what I was going to do or how I was going to make it happen, but down deep inside, I knew I needed to follow my gut. I later discovered this was called *intuition*.

Andrea didn't want me to leave New York. In fact, she thought it was a silly idea and assumed I wanted her to come with me. She had a good job and wasn't ready to leave the comfort of her big Italian family and head to California with no plan and no job. My father didn't support my decision either. Instead, he encouraged me to go back to school to get my teaching credential. I ultimately made the difficult decision to listen to *no one* and moved to California with my high school friend, Ted. I had no job lined up, and my only plan was to stay with my aunt and uncle and their two testosterone-driven high school sons. They lived up in the East Bay, right outside San Francisco. Ted and I planned the trip and set out to drive there in my 1987 yellow Ford Mustang. It was 1991.

The lesson here is to believe in yourself, and sometimes that requires blind faith. If you feel it in your gut and know deep within the fiber of your being that you are meant to do something or become someone, then believe it. Put yourself first. Rise above the expectations of society and even those of your loved ones. Find your mentors. Your inspiration. Women to follow and show you the way.

So, suddenly I was in California's East Bay with nothing but a degree in music and a guitar. I started a job with Western Reader's Service, where I met my next girlfriend, Nicole. Western Reader's Service sold magazines to poor people at astronomical prices. If it hadn't been for meeting Nicole, the job would have been a complete waste. She was amazing, and I fell in love with her. At nineteen years old, Nicole was confident, very feminine, and had a lot of style. She worked part time at Western Readers Service while she went to school full time at the Fashion Institute of Design and Merchandising in San Francisco.

I left Western Reader Service when I got hired by Enterprise Rent-a-Car. My job was to treat all these adjusters from car dealerships to lunch to entice them into using our car rental service. I had the *pleasure* of taking one Enterprise coworker along for lunch, whom I didn't think really liked me because he had never been particularly nice to me at work. Surprisingly, the lunch went extremely well, and I thought we were on our way to becoming fast friends. I had money left over from the company after paying for the lunch and he told me to keep it. I said, "Really?" He nodded, told me everyone does it, and not to worry about it. So, I kept the money. And he reported me. And I got fired. That dirty snitch didn't like me from the beginning and I knew it. I should have known that he was setting me up, but I didn't see it. That was my first lesson in politics.

The woman who fired me was the district manager, Claire. She sat me in her car that day and told me to sign a release in order to get my last paycheck. Claire stressed that it was really important, and then, in the same breath, she said, "Dina, please don't tell anyone at the company I'm gay." She was a lesbian and lived with a woman. I thought to myself: hook, line and sinker! I didn't sign the release, but I still got my fucking check. Later that day, I told Nicole how I negotiated with Claire to get my check without signing the release. I then said to Nicole, "Maybe I'll go to law school." I don't know what I was expecting her to say, but I wasn't expecting her to laugh in my face. And, just like that, her response triggered resentment. As the proverb goes, resentment is like drinking poison and hoping the other person dies.

I held onto that resentment and enrolled in the class I needed to take to study for the law school admission test (LSAT). That's where I met Lita Pettus, a young fiery Black girl from Oakland. I'd done horribly on the test, all because I have dyslexia, and the LSAT was a standardized test. Despite my miserable test results, I applied to a bunch of law schools but didn't get into a single fucking one. Lita called to say she got into the John F. Kennedy School of Law. I said, "Where the fuck is that?" It was in Walnut Creek, the next town over, so I said, "Good! How'd you get in? Because you did like two points better than me."

Lita said, "Dina, I think they let me in because of affirmative action. You need to call them up and tell them you're gay and hopefully they'll let you in." She gave me the dean's name and I called him to ask how gay people were supposed to change the laws if they couldn't even go to law school? The dean's only real response was that I needed to meet with him.

I went to the thrift store, bought a suit for the meeting, and then stapled it together because it was too big. My next stop was the law library in Oakland, where I pulled the prevailing case on homosexuality at the time, which was a United States Supreme Court case from 1986. The *Bowers vs Hardwick* case originated out of the state of Georgia, and it stated homosexuality was not a fundamental right. That was the law in the United States when I was applying to law school. I Xeroxed that case and memorized the whole fucking thing.

At the meeting with Dean Ken Meade, wearing a suit full of staples, I fucking argued that case like I was in the Supreme Court. The dean found my argument impressive and offered a conditional admission. At the end of the first year, I had to take a "baby" bar exam. If I passed, I could stay to complete the remaining two years of law school. If I didn't pass, I had to go. I said, "Deal!" And just like that, I was in law school.

You have to advocate for yourself when you're on your path. Get out and get experience. Do the hard work. Listen and learn from other people. The most important lessons I've learned throughout my career have been what *not* to do and who *not* to be like. The only way I learned was by doing and experiencing. There's no way to learn by experience if you barrel through everything and miss steps. You're missing the lessons that teach you what works and what doesn't. Start at rock bottom and move up. That's the best way to get the most experience. Those hard times and the plethora of mistakes will be the opportunities that shape your future.

Although I passed both the "baby" bar exam and the regular bar exam on the first try, when I moved down to Los Angeles I couldn't find a job. I was qualified to practice law, but I didn't have any experience. I knew how to play the guitar, sing, and manage a band but had no substantive experience with working in a law firm. I had to start at the bottom as a *free* intern for an entertainment lawyer in Los Angeles. When I wasn't working for free, I waited tables part time to make ends meet.

Several months later, the entertainment lawyer started paying me $15 an hour, but only if he could bill my time out at a higher rate to the client, and then only after they paid him. If the clients didn't pay, I didn't get paid simply because he wouldn't pay me out of his own pocket. A lot of the work I did wasn't billable, like opening his mail, getting his lunch, cleaning his office, and running errands.

His office was in Century City, and because the lawyer wouldn't validate my parking, I parked at Century City Mall and walked to the office. When I parked at the mall, it cost me $11 a day to go to work at my internship opposed to the $30 it would have cost me to park in the building. Neighborhood parking wasn't available, and if you dared to park on the street, you'd get towed. So, some days it was actually costing me money to be an intern.

I waited tables at night in West Hollwood until he was billing me out to clients enough times that I could support myself. I also had my mother's help. One of his clients was the Estate of Tupac Shakur. Tupac was shot and killed in 1996 while I was in law school. Lita was so upset the day he died, she left law school and went home.

A year into my internship, I went with my boss to a court hearing in downtown Los Angeles. Tupac died without a will or trust agreements, so the rights to his music were in dispute. Death Row Records claimed they owned all his unreleased music. The court had to approve all the business of his estate. I couldn't wait to meet Tupac's mother, Afeni Shakur, at the court hearing. She was going to be there with her sister, whom everyone called Aunt Glo, and Molly Monjauze, who'd been Tupac's assistant. When I saw Afeni in the hallway outside the courtroom, I marched right up and told her we had her finished report for the hearing. I said, "My mother told me all about you. You started the free breakfast program in the Bronx and wrote the ten-point program that's still in all the hospitals. And you ran a section of the Harlem chapter of the Black Panthers." Afeni looked to Molly and said, "Who the fuck is this girl?" And that was to say she loved me right away.

My boss really didn't really understand Black culture, and he didn't know Afeni at all. I occasionally heard him negotiating deals for the Tupac estate over the phone and I knew Afeni wanted to be involved. She's not the type of person who appreciates someone taking action without telling her, and then expecting her to approve. The boss was trying to negotiate a ten option deal with the record company for all the unreleased Tupac recordings, with the goal of getting Afeni a load of money. I knew that was the last fucking thing she wanted. It wasn't long before Afeni wanted me in the room every time there was a meeting.

One of the most important things I learned about being a lawyer, I learned from that internship. I learned what *not* to be like. The boss left the big firm he was at to start his own. I went with him, but now as a real lawyer. He partnered up with a big film lawyer, but that partnership quickly turned sour and they separated within two years. We then moved to the valley where I really began to recognize that *everything* he did was wrong. I started trusting my instincts, which is how I built my confidence. I was now a lawyer, not his intern, and I would argue constantly with him. He always reverted to, "I've been practicing law for twenty years, and you've been doing it for five minutes."

When Afeni found out he was paying me just $15 an hour, she fucking had a cow. Only then did he start paying me more, but I had to reimburse him for my office space, my parking spot, and a portion of the errors and omissions insurance, which is required for all lawyers in California. My monthly payment to work there was $1,710. I'll never forget it. $1,710 to sit in that chair. Afeni told him, "The only reason I'm here is because she's here," pointing to me. "If she's not here. I'm not here." My relationship with the boss became more challenging. I tried to make him happy, but I was also focusing on getting my work done and learning everything about copyright and music business deals on my own.

I had to work hard on a bunch of things so he could bill out my time to clients in order for me to earn more than $1,710. Of all the work I did, I struggled the most with hard copyright stuff, and he had no interest in teaching me. Just so I could learn enough for him to let me work on more, I took a music business copyright class at the University of Southern California at night taught by legendary music lawyer, Don Passman.

By the end of 2000, Afeni had nearly talked me into opening my own law firm. I remember thinking, "How is that going to work? I've only been a licensed lawyer for four years, and sober from alcohol for just three" (more on that later!). Sure, I *wanted* to quit my job, but actually *doing* it was a whole other thing. Afeni was relying on me more and more. I had already quit my waitressing job because I was finally making enough money at the law firm to make ends meet. Molly and I were also working with Ed McMahon on a TV show called *Next Big Star*. Ed McMahon was a client I got all on my own through one of the producers of a TV show featuring a girl group we represented called Wild Orchid. It was like *American Idol* before there was *American Idol*. Molly and I made sure the TV producers hired Tupac's friend, Staci Robinson, who, years later, Afeni hired to write the authorized Tupac Shakur biography. We were three peas in a pod back then: me, Molly, and Staci.

In March 2001, the Tupac estate released a double album called *Until the End of Time* through its company, Amaru Entertainment Inc. (Amaru was Tupac's middle name). Tupac had over one-hundred unreleased recordings when he died. He'd been shot in Las Vegas and died in the hospital days later. It was a lot of work getting the album cleared for release. We needed to make deals with all the original producers and songwriters. We also needed to make deals with the new collaborators Afeni wanted on the album, such as Lisa "Left Eye" Lopes from TLC and K-Ci & JoJo.

Because of the agreement for one of the post-humous albums, we had to run everything by Suge Knight, the owner of Death Row Records, despite that he was in prison. In 1997, he'd been sentenced to nine years on Federal RICO charges. This went on for months and months. All the while, my boss was putting more and more restrictions on me at the law firm because he was completely disconnected from what we were doing.

Later that year, I'd finally had enough. It was Yom Kippur, a Jewish holiday, when my boss didn't come into the office. He emailed me, saying he was raising my office rent, and that I had to start paying ten cents for every piece of paper I used in the copy machine. Molly reminded me that the Xerox machine was in my name and under my credit card because, when my boss had opened his new firm in the Valley, he didn't want to buy one because it was too expensive. Instead, he wanted us to go to Kinko's, a Xerox place, to make copies. That's how disconnected he was.

It was right then that I decided it was time to take Afeni's advice and open my own firm. No one was going to do it for me. I was already paying overhead, so why not just be my own boss? Afeni had already been telling everyone I was opening my own firm anyway.

David Cohen was the head of business affairs for Interscope Records at the time. He called me and said, "Afeni says you're opening your own law firm and that me and Jimmy [Iovine] need to help you. What do you need?" On September 27, 2001, with the help of my sober recovery friends, I wheeled the copy machine across Ventura Boulevard at 10:00 at night. I moved into the Amaru office on the third floor at Interscope Records on Colorado Boulevard in Santa Monica.

After spending a couple of weeks looking for office space, my friend from the recovery meetings who was also on the West Hollywood City Counsel at the time, John Duran, told me he just left a law firm that had a lot of extra space. He gave me the number of his ex-law partner, Joel Loquvam, who was a wills and trust lawyer. On October 11, 2001, I started renting space out of Joel's offices at 9000 Sunset Boulevard. I've been there ever since, but now I have all of Joel's space, too.

I spent a lot of years doing the grit work for that entertainment lawyer in Century City. I opened his mail, picked up his lunch and dry cleaning, and even blew up his kid's basketball. Whatever it took, I did it. You can't expect to get to the corner office and see only the shiny bells and whistles. A lot of things happened behind the scenes that got people to where they are now. They had to do some of the heavy lifting, and you'll have to do some of it, too. We all do.

There will be times you get rewarded. While sorting mail for that entertainment lawyer, I came across a flyer from Paramount Pictures that announced a Q&A event with the then-chairwoman of Paramount Pictures, Sherry Lansing, and a very famous author/actress, who at the time was sixty-five years old. I asked the boss if I could go and he said yes, so I registered and paid the fee. I was especially excited to hear Sherry Lansing. She ran a big movie studio, which I found amazing.

I went to the Paramount lot, where hundreds of other women were just as enthusiastic about being there for the session. I don't remember much about the talk, but at the end, Sherry said to the actress, "Now for the elephant in the room. All these women are dying to know how you look so good?"

This happened nearly thirty years ago, but I'll never forget it. The actress says, in her fabulous British accent, "Darling, the secret to looking so good is getting plastic surgery *before* you need it, so when you do need it, you don't actually have to get it. And you look like you never did it." I was thirty-four years old. It was a tip I'll never forget. Would that opportunity have come along if I'd said I was above going through that lawyer's mail? No!

Sometimes starting out at the bottom can be pretty shitty. A perfect example comes from an assistant I once hired. She said all the right things in the interview and had dreams of making it big in entertainment. After a few weeks on the job, she discovered that she didn't like it because some of her duties included cleaning up after my dog, Gatsby, who occasionally shit on the floor. She didn't want to do it. Not every part of a job is glamorous. Sometimes it involves a bit of "ruff" work.

Years of putting in all that hard work gave me a plethora of opportunities. I was told that if you aren't a straight white guy, or don't go to the right law school, or intern at the right law firm, or have famous parents, you're shit out of luck. But I believed in myself. I knew what I was capable of. I was going to work hard, starting at the bottom. And I wasn't going to give up. During those years, I also got sober. I put myself above my alcohol addiction. A predisposition that could have ruined my whole life. It wasn't easy, but it wasn't impossible either.

CHAPTER JOURNAL NOTES

- When was the last time you stood up for something or someone you believed in?
- Do you put yourself first? If not, who or what are you putting ahead of yourself?
- Are you willing to not listen to people who are holding you back?
- Can you arrange your life so YOU are at the forefront?
- Find ways to believe in yourself.
- Be open to training opportunities. Can you take a class or sign up for online tutorials? If so, what would they be?
- Be prepared to start at the bottom.
- Make a list of what you believe about yourself. What are your strengths? What do you need to work on.
- Make a list of what you can do to become that person.

3

Identify Your Triggers and Change Your Patterns

Everyone has triggers. They're emotional reactions to situations and people acquired from experiences, memories, or personal sensitivities. Triggers can be emotional booby-traps. When I'm triggered, I go down a rabbit hole and my intuition and emotional intelligence suffer. It's hard to be a power bitch when you're stuck in that sort of turmoil, but the trick is to identify the triggers and change the way you react to them.

I have gone to therapy and am a member of a 12-step recovery program for more than twenty-seven years. I learned that certain situations, words, actions, and events could become triggers, and that those reactions could become a liability to success. Some triggers include:

Negative past experiences, which can make you feel anxious, angry, or upset.

Challenges to personal beliefs and values, such as disagreeing or feeling defensive when someone or something clashes with your core beliefs.

Criticism or rejection, if you feel hurt and react defensively when someone provides feedback, such as a boss or partner.

Fear and anxiety, which can result from going through a traumatic event like physical, sexual, or emotional abuse.

Loss or grief, especially during significant dates like anniversaries or birthdays, which can intensify longing for security, connection, or recognition because those fundamental needs are no longer being met.

Comparison and envy, which creates a sense of inadequacy or resentment compared to others.

Change and uncertainty, which comes from fear of the unknown, especially if you are resistant to change.

The key to conquering a trigger is to recognize it and alter your approach in handling it. Because I grew up with an alcoholic family, the energy in the house could turn quickly, especially when my father got home from work. My mother kept a fun, creative, and inclusive energy going, but when my father got home, he was agitated and irritable and wanted peace and quiet. He would yell a lot if he didn't get it. Because of those negative experiences, I sometimes get triggered when someone's energy changes suddenly. It happens when a colleague abruptly cancels a lunch date and doesn't say why, or when someone I'm emotionally connected to doesn't return a text right away.

Instead of starting my *stinking thinking* ("I'm just not good enough" or "there's someone more important than me"), I learned not to take those things personally. I took the first step and identified the trigger. After learning that lesson, I gradually changed how I dealt with that trigger.

Another significant trigger for me was feeling judged and not being accepted, which stemmed from growing up gay, having a learning disability, and struggling with alcoholism. Later, being told that the law school I attended was "not an Ivy League school" insinuated that I still wasn't good enough. After achieving success and building a superwoman image, I used this persona as a shield to protect myself from the hurt I so often experienced from people who didn't accept me for who I was.

Because I felt judged, I guarded my trust against anyone whose beliefs didn't mirror my own, ironically adopting the same judgmental attitude I so vehemently despised. As a result, my defense mechanism was to either run from my perceived enemies or fight them, even without provocation. This response is a natural impulse we all experience at times. For people like me who want to make a difference and change their environment to a much more peaceful place, I had to understand how the opposite side really felt in order to empathize and recognize our similarities. However, learning this lesson came later in life for me.

I met Wendy Goodman in 2005. Wendy was beautiful, educated, from a good family, and on the same side of the political spectrum as I was. Wendy and I were together for almost eighteen years, married for fifteen of them. She was also in the music industry, working at RCA Records. It was our mutual friend Roger Widynowski, who also worked at RCA Records, who'd introduced us. Wendy had just transferred to the Los Angeles office from Dallas. She was in marketing and promotion. We hit it off and started dating. A few weeks into our relationship, we talked about our life dreams. I told her I wanted to be the biggest music lawyer in the country. She told me she wanted to have kids and be a mom. We were a match made in heaven, and just like good lesbians, we bought our first of three houses only six months into our dating relationship. My marriage to Wendy was great for a long time but then it wasn't. After my marriage to Wendy ended, I set out on the wild wild west of dating.

After spending nearly two decades with the same person, dating was foreign territory for me. In my hypnotherapy sessions and personal meditations, I focused on which *feelings* I wanted to experience when I connected with someone instead of creating a cliché checklist of characteristics and qualities they had, like attractiveness or a prestigious career. The four things I wanted to experience were safety, excitement, intensity, and passion.

About a year after Wendy and I separated, I started dating Sonia, a woman who had captivated my interest right away. She was smart and engaging and had a fiery personality. Her facial features and radiant smile could stop traffic. She was also *very* busy and career driven. This was a total turn on. Sonia was a police officer, and her sun sign was Scorpio. Although our dating situationship didn't work out, I learned so much about myself during that experience, especially in recognizing some of my emotional triggers.

One night over dinner, Sonia sprang on me that she had voted for Donald Trump. This set off a whole firestorm of emotions, as I consider myself a liberal Democrat and had focused on surrounding myself with like-minded people. Sonia and I had been casually dating for a few months, and yet her political stance had never come up, even though I regularly brought up the Democrat politicians I interacted with and the policy issues I was involved with professionally. She was also aware that Trump's "zero-tolerance" immigration policy led to the United States Immigration and Customs Enforcement (ICE) publicly seizing one of my high-profile rap clients, 21 Savage.

Sonia quickly went on to explain that she was a "moderate" and that I'd known this about her since we started dating. "Moderates don't vote for Trump," I said. "People who vote for Trump are Trumpers and far from being moderates."

She rationalized it by bringing up her unwavering belief in gay marriage and a woman's right to choose what she does with her own body. I jumped into an emotional rant about America's crazy two-party country and how we need to vote for policy rather than people.

I practically shouted at her throughout our dinner and interrupted her every time she tried to speak. The evening was pretty much ruined after that. Sonia took an Uber home that night, and we didn't speak for over three weeks. She'd challenged my deeply held personal beliefs, and this was a trigger for me. Usually, when someone did this, my pattern was to cut them out of my life. This was very different. Why? Because I *really* liked her.

I journaled about this experience and almost immediately recognized another pattern. What I discovered was that, when people I had a personal connection with challenged my beliefs, I cut them out of my life. But when it was a professional relationship or politician, I compartmentalized my feelings to keep them in my life. Why was this? I rationalized my response because they either paid me (i.e., a client) or were a congressperson or senator, and I needed their support for whatever legislation I was working on. That's when I realized I needed to change the pattern in my personal life if I wanted to have peace or, at the very least, have Sonia in my life.

Eddie Money was an American singer and songwriter, and ex-cop from New York City. He quit the NYPD in the early seventies because they wouldn't let him grow his hair long. He moved to California and quickly rose to the top after the 1977 release of his first album, which included the hits "Two Tickets to Paradise" and "Baby Hold On." Eddie came to me as a client after his long-time lawyer retired, but I had first met Eddie and his wife Laurie in Washington, D.C. We sat together at the Recording Academy's annual event, GRAMMYs on the Hill. The three of us quickly connected.

The Recording Academy is the music industry trade organization responsible for producing the Grammy Awards. Their voting members are Grammy award-winning recording artists, songwriters, producers, executive producers, engineers, and other creatives. Their non-voting members are music industry professionals like managers, agents, executives, business managers, and entertainment lawyers like me.

In addition to producing the Grammy Awards, the Recording Academy gets involved in advocacy issues that affect the rights of music creators like copyright and trademark protection, which are all federal laws. Copyrights are created when songs are written and then also when songs are recorded. GRAMMYs on the Hill is a two-day event where we visit members of Congress and the Senate advocating for the positions of music creators with respect to various legislative initiatives. The event includes a dinner and performance featuring Grammy Award-winning artists and musicians for all the politicians to enjoy. It's a fantastic schmooze fest!

At GRAMMYs on the Hill, a big-time music producer was pursuing me. I'd refused to take him on as a client after he sexually harassed me in Los Angeles. During the dinner event, he pulled a chair up beside me at the table. Laurie was on my other side and asked, "Who's this guy?" I told her the story and she immediately got up, went to the other side of the table, and told Eddie.

In no time, Eddie Money had become my bodyguard. He assertively escorted the producer away from our table and let him know he was never to contact me again. We spent the rest of the night talking, and the next day we were in the same group lobbying on Capitol Hill.

Eddie and I became fast friends. He was very protective over me and quickly incorporated me into his family. He loved Wendy and our sons and was the first person to teach the boys cuss words. Eddie was also a Republican, but that didn't seem to matter. We were like two peas in a pod.

Eddie's band included two of his sons, Dez on guitar and Julian on drums. His daughter Jesse was an amazing songwriter and a singer in his band. Laurie was the manager and ran the business. She'd grown up in Nashville surrounded by people in the country music industry, like Barbara Mandrell, and Johnny and June Cash. She graduated from the prestigious Belmont University with a degree in music marketing. In such a male-oriented business, Laurie took no shit from anybody. I loved her right away.

This family dynamic had all the makings of a great TV show. The modern-day *Partridge Family*. We worked up a deck and pitched the show concept to Mark Cuban, who was a majority owner of AXS TV at the time. Laurie tracked down someone who knew him personally, and once she got to him, she wasn't taking no for an answer, so they picked it up! Suddenly, I was the executive producer of the reality TV show, *Real Money*. We filmed just two seasons, as the second one was cut short by Eddie's esophageal cancer diagnosis. It was a devastating coincidence that both he and my mother were diagnosed with cancer around the same time. I introduced them over the telephone, and they became "chemo buddies," as Eddie called them. They called and texted each other almost every day. Sadly, Eddie passed away on September 13, 2019. My mother made it until 2022, when an aggressive form of leukemia finally took her. She died on December 3 in New York at 11:11 A.M.

Later that day, I called Laurie to tell her my mom had passed. She gasped and said, "Dina, oh my God, when Jesse and I were hiking today in Topanga Canyon, we saw two beautiful hearts in the sky that came out of out of nowhere!" When I asked her what time that happened, she said it was a little after 8:00 A.M. Pacific Coast Time. They'd taken a picture of the sky phenomenon. My family and Eddie's family were convinced that Eddie was waiting for my mother in heaven. They'd grown close, and I was their person. Who would have thought a right-wing ex-police officer from New York City and a liberal Democrat from Upstate New York could be two of a kind?

While journaling and meditating about my situation with Sonia, I committed to changing my mind about ghosting her just because she'd challenged my personal beliefs. I worked with my sister, Corinne, who is clairsentient and a wellness navigator in New Paltz, and she came up with a name for that particular trigger: The Eddie Money Rule, which means *co-existing in direct opposition.* So, now after Sonia and I reconnected and are close friends, every time politics comes up and the conversation starts getting a little sticky, one of us says, "Eddie Money rule," and the energy changes and we immediately pivot. Life is just too short.

Motivational speaker and self-help guru Mel Robbins talks about the "Let Them" theory. It's very simple: If the person you're dating says they don't want a commitment, then let them. If your employer doesn't recognize your value and keeps promoting other people, let them. Work on those things you can change and let go of the things you can't.

Also, look at your character defects—those pesky traits that limit your potential and hold you back. My character defects have changed over the years. Amongst all the defects, addictions stood out as the largest one. Addiction to alcohol, drugs, people, and sugar. Early in life, my character defects were co-dependency and seeking validation, which ultimately turned into constantly thinking I wasn't good enough. That one stayed with me throughout my adult life, it just went dormant here and there.

The first addiction I ever had was the TV series *Charlie's Angels,* with Jaclyn Smith, Farrah Fawcett,

Kate Jackson, and later, Cheryl Ladd. Where I grew up, there weren't many gays, and everything deemed "gay" was off limits. The New Paltz Catholics talked at length about how it was a sin. I wasn't into the lesbians they talked about around Moriello Pool, the ones who didn't take care of themselves and had loads of unkempt body hair, but I liked *Charlie's Angels*. They were feminine yet masculine, running around kicking the shit out of people with their high-heeled shoes. Yeah, that was my first addiction.

Like most addictions, *Charlie's Angels* was my escape. I needed a fantasy world to escape to because my reality was, "I'm not enough." I'm not good. Because I like girls, I'm going to hell. That TV series was my first addiction, meaning I wanted more, and I was obsessing over it. Episodes ran weekly from 1976 to 1981, long before the days of internet and streaming services. In my fantasy world, I pretended I was going out with these girls. That provided an escape from the reality where I feared becoming an overweight, hairy lesbian who was going to hell, yet it also triggered feelings of non-acceptance. Those feelings stuck around my whole life.

I had my first drink when I was thirteen. I stole it from my parents' liquor cabinet in the bar downstairs. And being immersed in music, my drinking lasted for a long time and was accepted as a normal part of my routine after I turned nineteen. When I started drink-ing, it was amazing. Also, I got into cocaine when I was eighteen. And that was even more amazing.

In every personal or romantic relationship I had, my drinking or using inevitably became a problem. My first girlfriend, Jill Stevens, would say, "Can you not drink tonight?" or "Maybe we can we have a drink or two and then leave?" All my girlfriends after Jill said the same sort of things. It always became a problem when I started drinking because, once I started, I couldn't stop. On the outside, I looked like I had it going on. I was a people person. Only the people closest to me didn't like it. My mother was con-stantly worried that I drank too much. She gave me my first "Big Book" of Alcoholics Anonymous when I was twenty-five years old, and I didn't get sober until I was thirty-two. There. That says a lot.

The reason she had that book is because she was in Overeaters Anonymous, and they use the same book. They just swap out the word alcohol with sugar or cookies. She coped with stress by sitting in the car and eating cakes during the day. She was obsessed with food, and my dad was a complete drunk. I could see that our family of five was trying to make the bad feel-ings go away. I never felt good enough, but those feel-ings went away when I drank. Suddenly, I was fucking great. I was pretty. I was accepted. All the hot girls at school wanted to be around me. And I thought, wow, this is amazing! The fun lasted for a long time, until it wasn't just fun anymore. It became fun with problems. And then it became just problems.

That's the first step in recovery—thinking of it as a problem. It's a hard first step because, a lot of times, you don't believe drinking is a problem since it's socially acceptable, so you rationalize it. When you're really hungover, you rationalize it by telling yourself, "Never again."

Being involved in the music industry, I noticed that drinking was even more prevalent compared to other fields. It was only a problem because other people were telling me it was a problem for *them*. It wasn't a problem for me until it became a *massive* problem for me. Fixing that was a series of steps. It didn't happen automatically, even though I dragged the Big Book around with me for years. Every time I moved, I brought it with me because it was like the spiritual thing I had, but I never really understood the magnitude of what it was.

A big part of what I did was compartmentalize people. When I got into law school, I had my study partner friends, my band, my girlfriends, and my druggie friends. Everybody was compartmentalized. Then my band got a residency at a women's bar, JR's Night Club, right in Walnut Creek where my law school was. Then *everyone* in my life started coming to my shows, and that was a huge struggle for me. One of our makeshift managers, Karen "Chew It" Smith, remembers taking me off stage and bringing me out to the parking lot for a chitchat. Because all these people wanted to hang out with me, she called it "Moses parting the sea" when I was done. I'd walk off stage and the sea of people parted, just like that. But I was so fucking stressed out because none of these people really knew me. I mean, they all knew a different part of me, and they each wanted that familiar piece. Alcohol became my bestie.

My study partners only drank after finals, which were every three months since we were on a quarter system. They drank at the bar where I did my residency. And then I partied with my drug-addict friends. And then with my band. If you put all that together, it meant I was drinking every day. Every. Single. Day.

After finishing law school, I learned that I passed the three-day bar exam on the first try in May 1997, and then on June 4, I was sworn into the California State Bar. I was now a licensed lawyer! Studying for the bar was no small feat. Having dyslexia, I knew it was going to be a challenge because a third of the exam was multiple choice, which was nearly impossible for me to overcome. I decided I needed a non-traditional strategy to pass that part of the test. The rest of the bar exam was right up my alley, persuasive writing.

My roommate at the time, Eddy Augustin, was interning with the Oakland A's baseball team while studying to become a sports psychologist. He used to tell me, "Failure is not an option!" One day, he came home from his internship and told me the team had contracted a hypnotherapist to work with the players who had anxiety on game day. It occurred to me that that was exactly what I needed to study for the bar exam! I started seeing a hypnotherapist and began *imagining* taking the bar exam.

Eddy told me how to bring about this mental manifestation. He called it "image-izing." He said to go down to Oakland where I would take the exam so I could visualize the building each night before I went to sleep. I took the exact train and bus route I would have to take three days in a row to get to the test site. I picked out the clothes I was going to wear each day and even planned what I was going to eat. I also ordered past bar exams from The State Bar of California website and took them under simulated exam conditions, timing myself with an egg timer. It all worked because I passed on the first try!

On June 9, 1997, my ex-girlfriend Jill's sister, Carrie Stevens, called me. She was Playboy's current

Playmate of the Month. I loved her. Years before, she had been Eric Carr's girlfriend which is how I ended up meeting and working with him in New York. She asked if I was an entertainment lawyer yet, and I said, "Yeah, since like four days ago."

Carrie said, "I miss you. Come live with me. You should be an entertainment lawyer here in Los Angeles." It didn't take me long to gather my shit, hire a moving company, and drive down to Los Angeles. Within a few weeks of Carrie's phone call, I was living in Sherman Oaks with Miss June 1997, and my entertainment law career was set to take off! Or so I thought.

I spent the next ten months of my Los Angeles career partying it up at the Playboy Mansion until my life became unmanageable. For the first time in twelve years, I didn't have college, law school, or a band to help me maintain a routine. The "I'm not good enough" mindset was fueling my addictions. Although I was a licensed lawyer, I couldn't find a job because I didn't have a lot of law firm experience.

Aside from working for a few months with music attorney Deena Zacharin in San Francisco while I waited for my bar exam results, I didn't have any experience on the legal side. I never had a mentor to tell me I needed to be an legal intern during law school to expand my learning and experience. And because I didn't go to an Ivy League law school or have any connections to Los Angeles entertainment lawyers, I was basically shit out of luck.

It didn't take long to realize all the music lawyers were white men. There were virtually no women except for Rosemary Carroll and Jill Berliner, neither of whom I knew personally or had any connection to, but I saw them both on a music lawyer list in *Billboard Magazine* when I was a musician in my all-girl band. Being a lesbian didn't help either. All of this contributed to the "I'm not good enough" stinking thinking that kept playing with my triggers.

Deena represented a bunch of cool bands in the San Francisco music scene, but she knew I would have more opportunities as an entertainment lawyer in Los Angeles, so she really pushed me to move there. When I told her I was too scared to go, she fired my ass. I didn't have a choice but to go then. Thank God for Deena Zacharin!

A couple of profound things happened during that period, which set the course for the rest of my life. Carrie did a segment on *Hard Copy*, which was an entertainment tabloid TV show like *Entertainment Tonight*. The segment was on Feng Shui, and they were filming at Carrie's apartment. Richard Webster, the author of *Feng Shui for Beginners*, was on the segment, too. While at Carrie's apartment that day, I met Richard's manager,

Anthony Benson, who said to me, "Carrie says you're looking for a job in entertainment law. Let me introduce you to our entertainment lawyer." And that's how I ended up interning for Major Penny-Pinching Buzzkill in Century City. Anthony called Buzz and begged him to take a meeting with me. I bullshitted my way through the interview that landed me the internship, thinking I was the one getting the good deal. I was really trying to learn, but it was hard to pay attention because I wasn't sober yet. I was still a mess.

Every time I hung out at the Playboy Mansion, I did something stupid. I got sloppy and started having blackouts. One night, I met the Playmates' stylist, Michael Holdaway, and he was fucking fabulous! He reminded me of Freddie Mercury from Queen with his leather pants, red shirt, and a magnanimous personality. Everybody wanted to be around Michael. He was infectious.

With my ginormous fishbowl margarita in hand, I tried to get him to do lines of coke with me in the bathroom. I still remember the way he shouted: "Girl, stop! I'm an alcoholic and I'm sober, eight years now! I don't drink or use drugs! Honey, put that away. And get that drink away from me."

I was fucking floored by his statement! Never in my life had I heard anyone announce, in public, at the top of their lungs, that they were an alcoholic. I had never come across someone so incredibly beautiful as this man. Or so extremely popular. By the end of the night, I was literally sobbing in his lap, confessing that I was an alcoholic, too. Needless to say, I'd embarrassed Carrie and some of the other Playmates. This was in February 1998.

That hadn't been enough to stop me though. I continued to drink. One night, I was in the limousine with Hugh Hefner, Carrie, and some other Playmates. We were on our way back to the mansion after having dinner at Dan Tana's in West Hollywood. As we were rounding the bend on Sunset Boulevard heading toward the Playboy Mansion, I fell against the door and then right out of the limousine and into the bushes. I was drunk off my ass. The experience was as much of a trauma as it was embarrassing. They literally didn't know what to do with me, because they don't call the police or an ambulance for anyone. They keep you at the mansion and take care of you.

Shortly after that incident, Carrie called and invited me to her house in Sherman Oaks. I had since moved into my own apartment in West Hollywood, across from Marix Tex Mex Cafe on N. Flores Street. I went to Carrie's house, where a few other women were there, some of them other Playmates. They sat me down, intervention style, and explained what my excessive drinking was doing to *them*. They all expressed their embarrassment over my drinking and said that if I didn't get it together, they couldn't hang out with me anymore. That was in March 1998.

I was still waiting tables and interning for Buzz-kill when my drinking became even harder to overlook. One early evening, I had my boss come meet me, Carrie, and the current Playmate of the Year, Victoria Silvstedt, at the Peninsula Hotel in Beverly Hills for drinks. I drank a bunch of vodka martinis that night. My boss paid the bill and, the next day at the office, he remarked on how much I drank and yet still walked out of there like I was fine and drove home. At that point, my tolerance level was sky high. He was shocked.

On another occasion, after work, Buzzkill told me I was going with him to the Conga Room because he was meeting some clients and needed me to take notes. The Conga Room was an upscale Cuban nightclub and restaurant on the Miracle Mile in a historic area of Los Angeles. My boss was an investor, and so were some of his Latin clients. He also represented the main owner of the club. My first thought was: "What the fuck did I do the last time I was at the Conga Room?" Jennifer Lopez used to go there all the time because her first husband was the manager. One night, she gave me a tango lesson.

I would go down there regularly with the Play-mates, and we would party our fucking asses off. They loved me there because I'd bring the Playmates and some of their other hot girlfriends. I'd drink my ass off and then not remember half the shit I did there. When Buzzkill said that's where we were headed, I panicked because I couldn't remember what happened the last time I was at the Conga Room, and I didn't have time to smooth things over if I'd gotten out of hand. Again.

When I got there, it was noticeably uncomfortable because people at the bar were saying, "Hey Dina! Come have a drink!" The boss found it very odd that nearly everyone knew me. He seemed rather uncomfortable as we passed through the bar to the restaurant area where some men were already waiting for him.

We all gave our orders, but I noticed I was the only one who'd asked for alcohol. As the dinner meeting dragged on, my focus wavered because I was becoming more preoccupied with the rate my wine was disappearing. I wanted another glass but felt weird about asking for one when the server came around. When I couldn't take it any longer, I excused myself to use the restroom, but I really just went to the bar and asked for two shots of tequila *immediately*. Some of the regulars wanted me to hang out, but I quickly excused myself and headed back to the table. After I sat down, with my back to the bar, my boss's jaw just about dropped. He was sitting across from me and watched a bunch of people from the bar come into the restaurant with tequila poppers, and they were screaming my name! He was, understandably, embarrassed.

After the meeting, I tried to explain and smooth things over as he walked me to my car. All he said to me was, "I don't want to hear your stories. This is a place of business for me, not a neighborhood bar where you just come down and hang out with your cronies and act like an ass. When you're here, you are an extension of me. But the problem is—you don't have the judgment to know better, and that jeopardizes my relationship with you."

In the rooms of recovery, they say that when you're ready to get sober, you have a *spiritual awakening*. I thought about all the times I put myself in danger or dire circumstances, and the people who tried to tell me I needed help. The signs were there, I just didn't see them.

The night of the Conga Room meeting, my life flashed before my eyes. That was April 18, 1998. On my way home, I stopped at Gelson's Market to buy a box of wine. After a few drinks, I found the liquid courage to call Michael Holdaway. He'd been trying to get me to go to recovery meetings with him since the incident at the Playboy Mansion, except I'd ghosted him and never returned any of his calls. That night, he was so happy to hear from me. I said, already a bit drunk, "I'm ready to get sober. I'm ready."

The next day, he picked me up and took me to a meeting at the West Hollywood Log Cabin. I haven't had a drink since. Michael Holdaway was my *Eskimo*, which is what they call the person who first brings you into the rooms of recovery.

That was my first time learning about triggers and the principles of the program of recovery. I applied a lot of what I learned there to fix issues in my professional life, because my career was the most important thing to me at the time. I needed to feel like I was enough, as industry leaders were already telling me I wasn't. Although I was determined to be successful, my biggest fear was that I wasn't any good at what I did.

I took a hard look at my life. At age thirty-two, I was a licensed attorney, but I was waiting tables at a café to support myself. I had also gotten arrested and charged with Driving Under the Influence (DUI) at the end of 1997, so I was going to DUI classes. I was interning for Buzzkill and not getting paid. The Playboy Playmates were telling me I was drinking too much. Drug and alcohol abuse rendered me powerless. All these things amalgamated into the hot mess that had become my reality. Once I admitted that my life was unmanageable, I began the twenty-seven-year-long healing journey to repair all the trauma in my life.

And then I got a new addiction. To success. And I went all in!

CHAPTER JOURNAL NOTES

- Pay attention to the emotions that upset or derail you. Recognize when they arise and how you handle the situation.
- These are your triggers. Write them down. Get to know them. Accept that they will not go away. Then, on the opposite side of the page, write what you will do differently compared to how you've usually reacted in the past. Change the pattern.
- Practice pausing when you feel these triggers. Take a minute and feel the emotion. Name it. Identify it as your trigger. Then, with intention, make a decision that you are going to commit to changing your reaction to it.
- By doing this, your triggers will no longer hold you hostage. They'll always be there, but you will recognize them and know how to change the way to react to them.

4

Tap into Your Intuition and Develop Your Emotional Intelligence

Women have intuition, otherwise known as a "gut feeling." Most of us are born with it, but we often ignore it. Some people say it like this: As women, we aren't immediately included in activities or opportunities that have traditionally included only men. For example, some sports, political offices, or positions in corporate industries. Because of this, women develop a deep sense of observation by becoming hypersensitive to the feelings and non-verbal cues of others, and we lose touch with our own feelings. Many of us are empaths. If it feels off or wrong, it probably is. Don't second guess your gut feeling because someone doesn't agree with you. Tell them to fuck off.

Emotional intelligence is having a sense of what will work and what won't because you can read and understand the emotions of people around you.

These two go hand in hand: intuition and emotional intelligence.

You can do a bunch of things to fine tune and develop your intuition and emotional intelligence. Take classes, learn about it. For me, besides getting sober, which gave me a heightened sense of clarity, I became knowledgeable in fine tuning my intuition through meditation and astrology. "Astrology is like a weather report; when you know it's going to rain, bring an umbrella," says Vedic astrologer Gurmeet Singh.

In Western astrology, finding out your sun sign, rising sign, and moon sign are important if you want to learn about aspects of your personality that seem natural and recognize the ones that seem challenging. Your sun sign reveals your identity, where you shine, and what fuels your ego. Your rising sign (ascendent) speaks to the energy you put into the world and how others perceive you upon entering a room. Your moon sign is where your body and emotions sit. My sun sign is Gemini, my rising sign is Scorpio, and my moon is in Gemini. Because I have learned the respective characteristics of these signs, I can navigate specific aspects of my personality. This boosts my confidence in some areas while making me proceed cautiously in others.

Gemini is an air sign ruled by Mercury, which is the planet of communication. I am intellectual and curious, and I have good communication skills. I'm also adaptable, sociable, and quick-witted. I excel at multitasking and have diverse interests and activities.

When I first got sober, I went to women's meetings in West Hollywood. Most attendees were lesbian. There was always lots of drama, and it was a fucking blast! Typically, after the meeting on Friday nights, someone would host a party at their home. I went with the group of women I hung out with most often. We were a tight-knit group because we all got sober around the same time, hung out together, and had a lot of drama together.

One evening, when we were hanging out in someone's living room, I noticed this beautiful Black woman with gorgeous braids. I saw her in the meetings sometimes. Her name was Karuana Gatimu, and she'd been sober longer than the rest of us. I asked what she did for a living, and she said she was a clair-cognizant. I said, "What is that?"

It means having a psychic ability to know things intuitively. For the next three hours, she shared the story of how she came to realize she had these psychic gifts. At first, it freaked her out so badly that she started drinking to block out all the energies she could read. She couldn't deal with it a lot of times. When she got sober, she realized it was a gift, and she started fine tuning it, so it became more prevalent.

Karuana explained that there are five main "clairs" or *senses*.

Claircognizant is "clear knowing" when you know something to be true, even though you didn't see it, hear it, feel it, or it hasn't yet happened. You just know it.

Clairvoyance is "clear seeing" or having visions or seeing images.

Clairaudience is "clear hearing" or the extrasensory perception where you hear messages that are otherwise inaudible.

Clairsentience is "clear feeling" where you feel sensations in your body.

Clairalience is "clear smelling" or the ability to perceive smells that aren't physically present. It's not as common as the other clairs.

Karuana realized she had this gift and began studying Western astrology, learning how to use tarot cards, and started a business giving psychic readings. It turns out she was pretty booked up and, I later discovered, pretty expensive, too!

When she does a client's reading, she looks up their astrology chart to see where their planets were when they were born, which tells her a lot about the person's planetary composition at that time. Using tarot cards, she has the client hold the cards while she clears the energy in the room with a meditation bowl. After a few minutes, as the client shuffles the cards, she clears the energy. She then has the client speak their name three times, and then she throws the cards out. And then she sits there and just tells them their shit.

As she explained what she did, I became obsessed with it and tried to figure out how I could come up with the money to book a session. When I turned a year sober, on April 19, 1999, my sober-girl posse pitched in and got me a gift certificate to Karuana! She did my first reading in June 1999, and I've been seeing her regularly ever since. Every single time one of my interns at the law firm took the bar exam, she told me whether they passed or failed before even they knew the results! She's also advised me on countless personal situations and relationships. She has literally been guiding me the entire time I've been sober. And she's usually spot on!

When my then-wife Wendy and I set out to adopt a child, the first adoption failed. Miserably. We had relocated the birth mother, Tina, from Texas to Los Angeles and put her up in an extended-stay motel near our house. About two weeks before she was expected to give birth, she changed her mind, left in the middle of the night, and went back to Texas. We were devastated. Wendy had endured emotional devastation before we explored adoption because she had already been through two artificial inseminations and three rounds of in vitro fertilization, none of which were successful.

Her life's dream was to have children, so it was all very hard on her. A few weeks after Tina was back in Texas, her sister called to let us know Tina was in labor. A few hours after the baby was born, she called again to say Tina decided to let us adopt the baby after all. We were ecstatic! We immediately called our lawyer, who told us it would be a near-impossible feat because adoption laws vary state by state, and in Texas, same-sex adoption was illegal. Horrible! Texas would rather put the infant in foster care than give him to lesbians.

Wendy nearly had a fucking nervous breakdown. That was in August 2012. In November, a new birth mother picked us to adopt her child, which was a pretty quick turnaround because, being Jewish and gay, we weren't getting picked very often. Being Jewish was worse than being gay because all these expectant women who were giving their kids up for adoption loved Jesus. Ironically, being gay wasn't really an issue unless the child was being born in a state like Texas, which is why we needed to bring the birth mother to Los Angeles to have the baby in California.

It was on Wendy's grandmother's birthday, November 17, 2012, when we received the news that we'd been picked again. And the woman was having twins! She was due on April 8, 2013. In January 2013, I had a reading with Karuana. She said, "Oh, my God, these kids are coming! You've got to get ready, energetically, mentally, and emotionally."

And I responded, "We are ready. We've got a double stroller."

She said, "No, no, no. I'm not talking about a double stroller. I'm talking about being *emotionally* ready, like your wife. She ain't thinking this is happening. And these kids are coming!"

I then told her we had time because they weren't due until April 8. We were in the middle of finishing up the baby room, which was going to be pink and blue because we were having a boy and a girl. At least that's what the sonogram said. But Karuana insisted they wouldn't be Aries kids, and not a boy and a girl. They were coming much sooner than April and would probably be Pisces. I took out the sonogram, showed her, and thought, "This time I'm going to prove Karuana wrong." But the twins were born six weeks early on February 27. They were Pisces. And they were both boys. Wilson Ray and Buddy Lee.

Karuana educated me about the twelve houses in the Zodiac. I learned that my eighth house of other people's money, royalties, commissions, banking, and finance had the good luck and communication planets of Jupiter and Mercury in it at the exact moment of my birth. At our first reading, she asked me what I did for a living. When I said I'm an entertainment lawyer, she said, "Oh, my God, that's a perfect profession for you. You need to trust your instincts."

This is why I started standing up to my boss at my internship. When he was fighting with Afeni, I would keep quiet because, back then, I was newly sober and had only been a lawyer for two years. I was also still struggling with my stinking thinking of not being good enough. After my sessions with Karuana, and understanding what Jupiter and Mercury meant in my eighth house, I found my confidence and started pushing back. That's when I began to trust my instincts.

Karuana taught me about all about the planets. You can learn a lot about a person when you know what their sun sign, rising sign, and moon is. When I get close to somebody, whether it's through a business or romantic relationship, I make a point of trying to find this stuff out. That knowledge gives me a bird's-eye view of how each person deals with things.

As a Scorpio rising, the world sees me as intense with a magnetic presence. Scorpio is a water sign, which means I have deep emotions, am sensitive, and have strong intuition. Because I'm aware of these Scorpio rising traits, I have developed a lot of confidence in these areas. Typically, women with Scorpio rising are powerful and have a strong will. They have a deep and sometimes a mysterious personality, and *trust me*, I play that up! Scorpio women can be highly preceptive, able to read between the lines, and understand the deeper motivations of others. I have a strong sense of purpose and determination, and because of this, I relentlessly pursue whatever goal I want to achieve. I tend to be guarded, but once I trust someone, I become fiercely loyal and deeply committed to the relationship, whether it's romantic, platonic, or professional.

With my moon also in Gemini, I am naturally and emotionally curious. I like to understand my emotional landscape as well as that of others. I express my emotions clearly and usually prefer to talk about my feelings in order to understand them, which is why I get a lot out of being in a recovery program and going to therapy.

On the other hand, I tend to be reactive and impulsive. I have to watch this carefully, as those tendencies have occasionally gotten me into trouble. Because I also have a high energy level and am always on the go, my restless nature makes it hard to relax. It took a lot of years to understand that I need to recharge my battery to really tap into my intuition and intellect. If I allow myself to recharge, I'm better equipped to adapt to changing circumstances and different people, and I can handle a variety of challenging situations. In other words, I am great in crisis.

I was representing a big rock band, and they were playing a show in Bogotá, Colombia. On show day, there were torrential rains, so the projected attendance was down about 40 percent. After the show, the band's gear was confiscated by whom we thought were the promoters and we did not know why. They wouldn't release any of our tour buses, which transported all our gear and equipment. The band had a show two days later in Buenos Aires, so the buses had to get on the road or the equipment wouldn't make it, and we would have had to cancel the show. The situation was dire, so I got into action.

I was part of a group called the International Association of Entertainment Lawyers (IAEL), and still am. This membership puts me in touch with lawyers all over the world. I reached out to a lawyer I know in Bogotá and told him what was going on. He went right down to the venue, which is how I found out what really happened. The promoter had to borrow money from a known drug cartel and couldn't pay it back because the show didn't do as well as he expected. He was under water by $100,000, so the drug dealers snatched our fucking gear that was split up between four tour buses. So, me and my lawyer friend in Bogotá spent the better part of the day negotiating with the drug dealers to get our tour buses released. We finally made it happen, and the band made the show in Buenos Aires, just in the nick of time.

My planets show that I can be good on my feet in challenging situations. Having a sun sign in Gemini, I'm a multitasker, very fluid, and I adapt to change quickly. A Scorpio rising is what makes me a fucking power bitch. Scorpio is a seriously powerful sign. Having a moon in Gemini allows me to process emotional things quickly and then move them into the places they need to go so I can power through.

I went through a similar situation with my client, 21 Savage, a prominent rap music artist. I met him because his agent and his then-label executive introduced me to him. They knew back then he was an immigrant and that I had some political influence so they figured I could be helpful. He was quickly rising to fame, and more and more eyes were on him.

He came to the United States from Great Britain when he was just six years old. His mother was from Dominica but lived in the U.K. and was a U.K. citizen. After they came to the U.S. she married an American man, acquiring her visa by way of marriage, and had more children. Savage's half-siblings were born in the United States, so they were U.S. citizens, but he was an overstay. He grew up in Atlanta as a Black immigrant, and in the Black community, you don't let anybody know your personal problems. Black people in America worry that the government will eventually use that information against them, as American history has demonstrated. So, he grew up in the shadows. He never really worked, like his friends who had part-time jobs, because he never had a government issued identification.

It was always a "play it close to the chest" thing until he became a prominent rapper. People started asking questions, and when someone becomes famous, their life becomes a spectacle. The record label executive, Celine, who was very close to him, was getting increasingly concerned about his immigration status. To make matters worse, Donald Trump had just been elected president. So now the House, the Senate, and the White House were all full of Republicans. People were freaking out.

Savage's music agent, Cheryl Paglierani, also told him he had to meet with me. Cheryl had said, "Dina's not only a music lawyer, but she has relationships in Washington, D.C., because she works on a lot of policy initiatives, and can probably be very helpful."

The first step was to get his visa, which was already pending. But you know, it's a process—a numbers game. In the meeting, I said I could call some very influential people and get that moving along. That's when he hired me. While I continued to get the visa process rolling, we also started managing all the music business-related work. On December 21, 2018, he released his long-awaited album, *I am > I was*, and it was an instant success. One of the album tracks, "A Lot," was released as a single. The song touched on family separation issues at the U.S.–Mexico border, which the press interpreted as a direct criticism of the Trump administration's policy on immigration. In January 2019, within days after he performed "A Lot" on *The Tonight Show Starring Jimmy Fallon*, I got a call from a high-level person in the White House who said United States Immigration and Custom Enforcement (ICE) was looking into taking Savage. I freaked out and called him immediately, telling him he had to come to California because it's a sanctuary state. He didn't want to come because he was playing at the Pepsi arena that night with J. Cole. Atlanta was also hosting the Super Bowl that weekend, and he had a VIP sideline seat.

I flew Danielle Price from my office to Atlanta immediately. Not only because she was a fabulous lawyer but also because of her high level of emotional intelligence. While she was in Atlanta, I started working behind the scenes with my contacts in Washington, D.C. I instructed Danielle not to leave Savage's fucking side, and to get him on the plane right after the Super Bowl. That was the plan.

Another thing about Savage, because of his immigration status, he had never flown commercial. Every flight he'd taken had been on a private plane. It was hard for him to agree where to play shows, and everybody thought he was just picky about where he performed, but it was only because he couldn't fly commercial.

Danielle flew to Atlanta on a Thursday. She spent all day Thursday and Friday with him and had no issues. She went with him to the show at the Pepsi arena. That night, as I was lying in bed, my phone rang at 10:00 P.M., which is not good because that's 2:00 A.M. in Atlanta. It was Danielle. Very calm and methodically, she explained that, as they left the venue, the entire crew was pulled over. ICE was there, and they took Savage away.

I literally hung up the phone and, for the next nine days, I fucking called every high-level member of Congress I knew and got them involved. His business manager, Sally Velazquez and I also hired one of the most prominent immigration lawyers in the country, Charles "Chuck" Kuck. Congresswoman Karen Bass, who later became the mayor of Los Angeles, was the Chairwoman of the Congressional Black Caucus at the time. I told her what was going on, and she said she'd get behind it. She wrote a letter of support on behalf of herself and the Congressional Black Caucus.

I met Congresswoman Zoe Lofgren from Silicon Valley when I was working on copyright reform with the House Judiciary Committee. At the time, she was considered the music-industry nemesis because she represented the district where the streaming and technology companies were located. The music industry was at war with them because they weren't compensating songwriters properly. Her reputation as a formidable opponent in copyright discussions preceded her. People in the music industry were intimidated by her pointed questioning during hearings. She's a force to be reckoned with. Someone who doesn't take any shit. She scared the fuck out of everybody in the music business.

Zoe was also the Chairwoman of the Immigration and Citizenship Subcommittee in the House. Chuck knew her pretty well. I had already testified in Congress on a couple of other judiciary initiatives, so she knew me. Not well, but she knew who I was. She agreed to have dinner with me, so I flew to D.C. to meet with her.

She'd done some research on 21 Savage and said her kids warned her that he's really violent. I said, "Wait a second. Wait, what?" It didn't take long to realize Zoe had no connection to music, so it made sense that she didn't understand it, let alone rap culture. She didn't grow up listening to music and didn't play music. Her husband and kids weren't into music, so there wasn't any music ever playing in their home.

Her questions on copyright reform started making sense because she was completely in the dark about music. She just didn't know. Some kids grow up not playing sports, so it's no surprise when they know nothing about sports when they get older. This family simply knew nothing about music.

I spent the next three hours educating Congressmember Lofgren about the political and cultural relevance of rap music in America. Afterwards, she said, "Oh my God, this is amazing! And fascinating! Can you put that in a memo for me and my staff?" I said I would and then worked on the memo on the flight home. Within a couple of days, I submitted the memo to the Congresswoman's chief of staff. That memo was the basis for her publicly coming out as Chairwoman of the Immigration and Citizenship subcommittee and condemning ICE and the Trump administration for taking my client, 21 Savage. Through the combined efforts of Congressmembers Zoe Lofgren, Karen Bass, Maxine Waters, and a close friend of both mine, Chuck's and Savage's, Congressman Hank Johnson in Georgia, we stopped 21 Savage from being deported and now, years later, he has his permanent green card.

In my opinion, using astrology to identify your strengths and weaknesses really gives you the upper hand in business. Twelve houses exist in Western astrology, and everyone has them. At the time you were born, there were specific planets stationed in each of these houses. This marks your "planetary makeup." If you understand the houses and those planets, you can capitalize on your strengths and work on your weaknesses.

In a nutshell, the 12 houses are:

First house: Public perception, or how the world sees you

Second house: Personal income and work ethic

Third house: Communication

Fourth house: Home and family

Fifth house: Romance, love affairs, and self-expression

Sixth house: Health and fitness

Seventh house: Marriage, business partners, and contracts

Eighth house: Other people's money, royalties, and commissions

Ninth house: Higher education, publishing, religion, and travel

Tenth house: Career and reputation

Eleventh house: Friends, groups, and aspirations

Twelfth house: Endings, karma, closure, and spirituality

The ten planets in Western astrology each have meanings, unique qualities, and characteristics:

The Sun is the Planet of Self, which represents your
   personality and ego. (It's your identity, your face
   to the world)

The Moon is the Planet of Emotions

Mercury is the Planet of Communications

Venus is the Planet of Love and Money

Mars is the Planet of Passion

Jupiter is the Planet of Luck

Saturn is the Planet of Karma and Discipline

Uranus is the Planet of Rebellion

Neptune is the Planet of Illusion

Pluto is the Planet of Power

I believe that knowing where all these planets
are at the time of your birth is an important insight
to study and understand. I have the planets Jupiter
and Mercury in my eighth house of luck and money.
Those are strengths, especially in business. However,
one challenge in my chart is having the worker-bee
disciplinarian planet of Saturn in my fifth house of
romance and love affairs. As I became educated in
astrology and my chart, I had to hyper-focus on learning how to be present in romantic relationships. This
didn't come as naturally to me as negotiating a record
deal. I didn't understand how to really show up for a
romantic partner. I do now because I have been working on it for over twenty-seven years, which is one of

the other influences of Saturn, bringing opportunities for self-discovery and growth.

A few years after I got sober, I was dating a lawyer who lived in Marina Del Rey. One morning, after staying over at her house, she made me a romantic breakfast on the beach. She told me not to come out until she called me, and when she did, I came out with my fucking work bag full of contracts! She was extremely upset, and for the life of me, I couldn't figure out why because *I was there.* It was because I was going to sit on the beach during this brunch and read all my contracts. It never dawned on me that I wasn't present or engaged.

Once I understood that I had challenges in that house, I learned how to be present. Even when I was married, and we had date night, I had to be very intentional about it. I had to make sure all my business was completely taken care of, so I didn't end up bringing my work-related emotions and preoccupations along for the date. Then I had the space to turn off and connect for the date night.

Saturn, the worker-bee planet, is very powerful. People born with Saturn in their fifth house have a positive outlook toward their work and are highly dedicated to it. When I'm enjoying myself, a guilty part of me thinks: *Shouldn't I be working? What am I doing having fun?* Having Saturn in my fifth house of romance, love affairs, and expression is challenging. If I had Venus in my fifth house, oh man! Venus is straight on love, but I've got fucking Saturn.

I also have Mars in the seventh house, and Mars is the take-action planet. In addition to marriage, the seventh house is also the house of business partners and contracts. Another attribute of Mars is intellect. The advantages of a quick-thinking mind are thinking on your feet, understanding complex situations, and being able to read a room with ease. These are things that really helped me navigate in the 21 Savage situation and, on a daily basis, help me negotiate deals for my clients, especially in high-pressure scenarios.

Neptune is in my first house. This planet is fluid and changeable, so when I need to see both sides of a situation, I can do that. I understand the world is emotionally intimate, and everybody has feelings about everything and that resonates with me. The first house is the house of public perception. It's how the world sees you. Neptune also has its showier side, as it rules creativity, movies, fashion, and all forms of glamour. That's how so many people describe me by saying, "Dina makes me feel really important" or "I really feel as though Dina cares about me" or "Dina is always fashion forward!" My first house has provided me with opportunities to connect with a variety of people and show them that I genuinely care about their feelings and interests. There is also a shadow side to every planet, and in Neptune it represents drugs and alcohol addiction and escapism. These are the obstacles I've worked tirelessly at to overcome.

Having a high degree of emotional intelligence gives me a leg up in reading the room and assessing a situation. The U.S. is a two-party country, Democrat and Republican, which means citizens have to prioritize their issues. If your top priorities include a woman's rights to choose (i.e., abortion rights), affirmative action, climate control, and LGBTQ+ rights, then you have to vote Democrat. Even if Republican politicians believe in those things as well, they have to vote down party lines, or they don't receive fundraising support from their party when they're up for re-election. In the U.S., it's nearly impossible to be re-elected without support from either the Democrat or Republican party.

There are also Republican issues and some of the big categories are the right to bear arms (own and carry guns) without much regulation, freedom of speech, and controlling their own property rights without government regulation. Well, believe it or not, copyright is a Republican issue. Why? Because it's a *property right.* Property rights are real property (i.e., a house), copyrights, and trademarks. Specifically, copyrights and trademarks are called *intellectual property rights*. Under the first Trump administration, we had an opportunity to pass much-need copyright reform. After all, the White House, the Senate, and the House of Representatives were *all* controlled by the Republican party at that time.

Although the liberals felt it was a dire time, we had a limited opportunity to pass some real copyright reform. For the better part of two decades, streaming services disrupted the music industry. In 1999, when Napster and Pandora came along, the demand for compact discs dissipated. Within the next ten years, all these interactive streaming services like Spotify and Apple Music popped up. Suddenly, no one was buying CDs. None of the providers were properly compensating music creators either.

In 1998, there was a law passed called the *Digital Millennium Copyright Act*, which created a public performance right and payment to music artists for only *non-interactive* digital streams of sound recordings. *Non-interactive streaming* means internet radio and Sirius radio in your car. These are the platforms the consumer could *not* interact with, like creating playlists. It was a "new" intellectual property right, which was good because it created a new income stream for music artists, producers, and sound-recording owners (i.e., usually record companies). But there were no laws for *interactive* digital services like Spotify and

Apple Music. The difference between *non-interactive services* and *interactive services* is technical, but there's a very important distinction.

These new interactive services made deals to stream recordings directly with record labels, but not the publishers or the songwriters. There was a little protection overall, but there was no protection for songwriters. So, the service providers streaming music weren't compensating songwriters. It was a shit show.

I had the opportunity to work alongside Congressman Doug Collins, a Republican from Georgia. Congressman Collins was a pastor before he became a congressional representative, and he holds a strong right-wing conservative stance. But he and I got along just fine. I don't know why we did, but our professional relationship just worked.

In 2017, Congressman Collins called me while I was in a rehabilitation facility recovering from a cervical discectomy and anterior fusion resulting from an infection in a neck disc that turned into deadly bacteria and that nearly took me out. It was in April right after my nineteenth sobriety birthday, and I was on tour with deadmau5. The morning of his New York show, I woke up with a pain in my neck which was so bad I decided to fly back to Los Angeles the next morning. The plan was I was going to see my chiropractor and then I would meet deadmau5 (real name: Joel Zimmerman) back out on the tour after that. After seeing my chiropractor in Los Angeles, it just got worse. I never returned to the tour but instead I was just going to stay in Los Angeles and see him at his show here. The evening of the Los Angeles show, his business manager, David Weise, picked me up. Everyone was very worried about me because I couldn't turn my neck without being in excruciating pain. After a series of seeing doctors and getting tests, no one could really figure out what was wrong with me. The only thing I could do to alleviate the pain was to sit upright and try to lift my head up off my shoulders.

The next day, one of my friends in recovery, Steve Longo, called Wendy to check on me. She told him I was not good and asked him to come take me to the ER. She did not want to call an ambulance because the boys were only four years old at the time, and they were already stressed and worried. Thank God, Longo took me to the emergency room because shortly after I was admitted and undergoing tests, I went into septic shock. The main doctor in charge of me in the emergency room, Dr. Ariella Morrow, had the emotional intelligence to immediately bring on an infectious disease doctor to study my MRIs and he determined that I had a bacteria traveling rapidly down my spine.

They brought in an orthopedic surgeon, Dr. Terrence Kim, and admitted me for immediate surgery. I ended up staying in the ICU for a few days, with my sobriety sister, Ginger, staying overnight with me until I was ready to be transferred to a regular hospital room. Meanwhile, Wendy was trying to manage everything at home with the kids and updating all our family members and my close clients. One of my colleagues, Lou Taylor and her husband Rob, a pastor in Nashville, held a daily prayer circle for me.

After I got out of the hospital, I went to the California Rehabilitation Center to relearn basic skills like walking, keeping my balance, and washing my hair. Little did I know it was going to be almost six months before I was physically able to return to the office.

When Congressman Collins called to check on me, he told me he had some upcoming meetings with the publishers about creating a new law, but he wanted to have direct relationships with the songwriter community, not just their music publishers. He gave me some ideas and I sketched out some things the songwriters needed like an independent non-profit to collect and pay out songwriter royalties (currently it was the record companies paying songwriter royalties), having songwriters on the board of that non-profit, and audit rights. Working with David Israelite and the National Music Publishers Association, our collaboration turned into the *Music Modernization Act*, which was passed unanimously in the House, then it passed in the Senate, and then signed into law by President Trump himself in October 2018.

Over the years, I've learned how to talk to the different Democrat and Republican representatives to make things work. Ultimately, you need both sides to pass a law. In 2018, the White House, the Senate, and the House of Representatives were all Republican and because copyright is a Republican issue, they made it a huge priority. Usually Republican and Democrats are not aligned on a lot of things but back then they all agreed on this much needed copyright reform.

I would grab Eddie Money, and we would schlep our asses to Washington, D.C. Bringing Eddie along for the ride meant I could get into these Republican offices. They don't see your ass unless you're part of their party. During the lobbying for the *Music Modernization Act*, I fine-tuned all my talking points and negotiation skills to address the perspectives of both sides. With the Republicans, I emphasized the importance of property rights, stating, "This is our property right." They responded positively because Republicans love property rights. I then noted, "We cannot negotiate effectively in a free market," to which they again agreed, because Republicans love free market negotiation. Additionally, I pointed out that the government regulates our copyrights. This resonated with them because they fucking hate government regulating their property. That's how we got their votes.

I'd then go across the hall to the Democrats and say, "We're poor songwriters, we have no health insurance, and we don't have a songwriter's union." That's all it took to get their vote. And the next thing you know, we had a unanimous vote in the House.

Mars is my intellectual take-action planet. Neptune is my read-the-room planet. Gemini is my ability to multitask, and with Mercury in my eighth house, I'm a great communicator. What do I say? And what don't I say?

Understand the landscape. Know your audience— the people you're speaking to. Use your gut and intuition to determine what you're going to say. Read the room by paying attention to the energy and temperature of the people in it, and the timing.

Understanding my planets and houses helped me understand how I work best and what I still need to work on. That knowledge is a great tool and has helped me up my intuition and emotional intelligence to another level. You have the same ability. Get busy.

CHAPTER JOURNAL NOTES

- Think of a time when your intuition guided you in a decision. What was it?
- Get connected to your gut and notice your behaviors. Can you make the correlations?
- What practices help you stay emotionally grounded and in tune with your instincts?
- If you're curious about your astrology chart, plenty of apps are available for download. The ones that I like are the Chani app, Co-Star, and The Pattern. Getting started is as easy as entering your birth date, place of birth, and the *exact* time you were born.
- Learn about the 12 houses and what each of the planets represent.
- How does the placement of planets in the different houses at the time of your birth affect your personality's predispositions?
- This will come with a lot of practice. Over time, you'll become connected to your emotions, and you'll also recognize emotional cues in others.

5

Take Action!
Shit, or Get off the Pot

Nothing changes if nothing changes. You have to get into action and actually do the work! No one can do it for you. Getting it done is *much harder* than it sounds. It could mean quitting a job, breaking up with a long-term partner, moving to a new city, going back to college, or taking any other giant step toward living your dream. Making difficult changes and being determined to overcome obstacles requires a deep commitment to personal growth and resilience. It involves facing fears, pushing through doubts, and embracing discomfort as a catalyst for transformation.

Most people complain and never do anything. My friend and colleague, Willie "Prophet" Stiggers, Chairman of the Black Music Action Coalition, always asks people, "Do you want to be a thermometer, or do you want to be a thermostat?" A thermometer is always going up and down, depending on the temperature of the room, whereas a thermostat *sets* the temperature in the room. The thermostat is in control, whereas a thermometer is controlled.

In 1997, when I moved to Los Angeles from Northern California, I had an opportunity to work for an insurance defense law firm as an attorney. My uncle, a bigwig for Xerox at the time, had pulled some strings and got me a job interview at a firm in downtown Los Angeles. I probably could've had that job. The job offered a competitive salary, complete with health insurance and a cell phone allowance.

Instead, I opted to intern for free at Buzzkill's firm and waited tables. As a licensed attorney, waiting tables was humbling, at best. To learn the ropes of music law, I had to take action. No one was going to do it for me. Obstacles are not roadblocks, but opportunities to learn and grow stronger. Through unwavering determination and focus on the end goal, even in the face of adversity, I emerged from the challenge with newfound strength and a deeper understanding of myself.

Similarly, when I got sober in 1998, I had to admit that I was powerless over drugs and alcohol, and that my life had become unmanageable. I had to take action. No one was going to get sober for me. I had to be the one to decide it was time to start going to the 12-step recovery meetings. Those early days of sobriety were challenging, but I was determined to stay sober under any circumstance, and I was counting days. Every day without alcohol gave me a new sense of hope.

I started going to recovery meetings Monday through Friday at 7:30 A.M. at the West Hollywood Log Cabin. Then I'd drive to my internship. If I didn't have to go straight to my waitressing job at night, I went to another meeting at night with my Eskimo, Michael Holdaway, and the posse of newcomers he was sponsoring. Afterwards, we hung out at someone's house or a restaurant in West Hollywood called the French Market. On weekends, I went to the women's meetings with my posse of newly sober lesbian friends. We all encouraged each other to stay sober. Some of us did, some did not. Some passed away. For me, it was all a commitment to *myself.*

Being committed to yourself means being brutally honest with yourself—straight-up honest and truthful *about* yourself and *to* yourself. In addition, you may have to ask hard questions of others and be prepared to hear answers that may be painful. This is what allowed me to get a divorce from a woman I loved. Many people choose to stay in marriages out of fear of the unknown or the comfort of familiarity, making divorce a daunting prospect. Generations past, people stayed in passion-less marriages. This was the marital practice I grew up witnessing. Being honest with myself and asking Wendy to be honest with me is what allowed us to take the action necessary for us to both be happy.

As I said, when Wendy and I met, she had a prominent marketing and promotions job at a record label. The first album Wendy worked on at her first record company label job was Alanis Morissette's *Jagged Little Pill*, so that was her barometer for success. That album was nominated for nine Grammy Awards, won five, and had sold millions and millions of albums. After working for that label, Maverick Records, which was owned by Madonna, she eventually went to work for Clive Davis, a legend in the music industry.

Clive started as a music lawyer working in-house at Columbia Records. He eventually transitioned from the legal and business affairs department to become the president of CBS Records, and he's been credited with finding some of the biggest stars in the business. He produced a lot of their records, too. Some of his most notable signings are Janis Joplin, Aerosmith, Bruce Springsteen, Billy Joel, Earth, Wind & Fire, Barry Manilow, Aretha Franklin, Dionne Warwick, Whitney Houston, Usher, TLC, P!nk, and Alicia Keys. Wendy and I met a few years after I opened my law firm, and I was working hard on trying to get my name out there. I'd been sober for seven years. In the recovery community, they say "it takes five years [of being sober] to get your marbles back," so I had only gotten my marbles back a couple of years earlier.

Not only was Wendy self-sufficient through her own contributions, but she was also respected and well-known in the music industry. That was new for me. Some of the women I used to date were musicians just trying to get record deals and had no real jobs or income. Wendy was the full package. Her life's dream was to have kids and my life's dream was to be a successful and well-known music lawyer.

Wendy's grandparents were some of the most influential people in my life during those days. They retired from the clothing manufacturing business in New York City and were living in the penthouse of the Fairmont Hotel in Newport Beach, California. I thought, "This is how I want to retire. Living in the penthouse of a five-star hotel with everyone kissing your ass." Her grandfather was a financial savant who played the stock market daily with his broker at Fidelity. Her grandmother, who they called Mowie, was cultured, refined, and always put together, even on her deathbed. She passed away on July 5, 2016.

Mowie was well-educated and obsessed with classical music and the opera. Because I had studied classical music in college, she loved me! Wendy and I regularly took her to the Opera at the Dorothy Chandler Pavilion in downtown Los Angeles, and then out to dinner at one of her favorite restaurants. Wendy and her family were Jewish, liberal, and spicy! She even has a gay brother, Michael, who is also in the music business. Having grown up with parents from the Borscht Belt in Upstate New York and knowing as much about the Jewish culture as I did, it was a match made in Heaven.

Wendy and I decided to get married in 2008 and immediately started planning the whole thing. As coincidence would have it, in May of that year, the United States Supreme Court had deemed a state's ban on same-sex marriage unconstitutional, making California the second state to legalize gay marriage. Wendy and I got married over the Labor Day Weekend that same year.

We had no idea our marriage would be legal . . . in California, anyway. It was still odd though. Despite being legally married in California, our marriage remained unrecognized by the Federal government. To further complicate the shit, and thanks to the Knights of Columbus and the homophobic Catholic Church, in November 2008, California voters repealed the law and amended the state's constitution to, once again, ban same-sex marriage. We were in limbo, but we still considered ourselves married no matter what the law said.

Right before our twin boys, Wilson and Buddy, were born in February 2013, things were very busy. Besides Wendy traveling all the time for work, I was also managing Steven Tyler, in addition to being his lawyer. I was in a very public lawsuit with his ex-manager. I was also trying to balance my relationship with Afeni Shakur, because she was used to having me on speed dial and could summon me down to her farmhouse in Lumberton, North Carolina, at a moment's notice.

Around the seventeen-year mark in our marriage, both of us had grown apart emotionally. We just wanted different things, so we got into action. My option was to stay in a passionless marriage, because that's what my upbringing taught me to do. You stay together. After all, it's supposed to be *for better, for worse . . . until death do us part*, like my parents and grandparents did. Or we could choose personal happiness and separate. I didn't know what that would look like. Would we be happy apart? There were a lot of scary unknowns.

One particular event kind of solidified our choice. Wendy and I decided to go on a date night. We had our nanny, Angela, stay with the boys while Wendy and I checked into a fancy room at the Beverly Hills

Hotel using a holiday gift card I received from one of my clients, deadmau5. Our date night was awesome. We ordered room service and watched Netflix for five hours.

The next morning, we decided to get into therapy. The therapist asked those extremely difficult questions. After a few months, Wendy and I realized that although we loved each other very much, we weren't "in love" with each other anymore, and it was time to "consciously uncouple," a term made famous by Gwyneth Paltrow. That took a lot of strength and perseverance. After talking with the therapist about how we were going to separate, we finally decided when we'd do it. We first flew to New York to tell my family and then we told Wendy's family before telling the kids. I moved out of our family home in July 2022. It took a lot of personal strength for us to decide what to do. Our happiness required us to take action. Standing still was not an option. Wendy had been unhappy for a long time, and I knew it.

Around this time I was becoming emotionally attached to someone new in my life, a woman named Maria. Having been in a recovery program, I learned that it's always principles before personalities, which means you have to be honest in all your affairs. Lead an honest life. First, I had to acknowledge to *myself* that I was attracted to and wanted to be with someone else. After I told my recovery program sponsor and therapist about it, I was open about it with Wendy. Understandably, she was very hurt, but despite that, we had conversations about it with honor and integrity. Once I moved out of the house, I could tell that woman how I felt. I had to act on my truth.

Maria was straight as an arrow. Not even bi-curious. She said, "I'm really flattered. But as much as I'd like to be a lesbian because men make me crazy [she was divorced], I'm straight." I had a hard time with this at first. After all, I had just left my marriage of eighteen years, but I recognized through meditation, journaling, being in therapy, and talking with my sister, that it was meant to be. The universe was tapping me on the shoulder. It was time to take action.

The biggest lesson I learned from that experience is to have faith, even when things don't go your way. In fact, that's the very reason you need to have faith. Even though Maria and I were never romantic, she became a very close friend of mine. Another gift from the universe. This ultimately got me out of a marriage that wasn't working for either of us. Looking back now, the Maria situation had to happen in order for me to take action, or I never would have.

Being honest is a choice. If you sit and wait in complacency, you risk becoming dishonest in the future. Most people don't take action, and then they do destructive things and develop dysfunctional and toxic behaviors. That karmic energy then bleeds over into other areas of life. It creates a toxic energy. Once you start cheating on your spouse, you begin a pattern of dishonesty and living without integrity. Then what's next? You relapse on drugs and alcohol? Start living a life of lies? And then you've got to cover up those lies. That all leads to toxicity. And then suddenly, when you thought you were an emotionally, spiritually, and mentally healthy person, you look in the mirror and see that you're not healthy anymore. You're lying to your spouse, children, friends, colleagues, and yourself.

I realized that if I was feeling an attraction to Maria now, it would happen again with another woman in the future. I knew, without a doubt, that I would want to be romantic with someone else. That was the hardest truth for me to face.

I didn't get sober to be miserable, and we recognized that our marriage had run its course. It was time for both of us to pursue happiness. We were both entering the last stages of our life—the last thirty years or so—so, I asked myself, what am I going to do? Stay and not be happy or take a risk and maybe be happier?

Starting over is harder when you're older. You don't want to waste a lot of time. Younger people might hold on a bit longer, or they'll lie to themselves longer. They're more hesitant to shit or get off the pot.

It takes a lot of strength to take action. Fear takes control. They question: "What am I gonna do?" or "How am I gonna do this?" Eventually, those questions turn into ineffective solutions like "Don't do it," keeping things as they are. It's comfort, it's fear.

Then other things happen. They start drinking too much, gaining weight, and self-medicating. People get complacent, and they get used to complaining. As those toxic behaviors seep into their way of life, they become more and more miserable without even realizing it. If this is the person you've become, you've got to take an action. Nothing changes if nothing changes.

My dream was to be one of the best entertainment lawyers in the country. I could fantasize about it, or I could take action. The legalities of the music business are extremely complicated, and I was working at a place where no one had any desire to teach me anything. If I was going to learn, I had to figure it out on my own, which is why I enrolled in Don Passman's music business class at USC. I was fortunate to have him as a mentor. His influence on me was immense. He authored *All You Need to Know About the Music Business*, which is like the music industry bible. That book breaks down all the different relationships and deals in the music business. Don covered everything in the book during class. It was incredible, and years later, I modeled my UCLA music business class after his. In fact, his book became the required reading for my class.

When I started at Buzzkill's firm, it was hard for me to absorb the material. It was a complex task, and I desperately needed to grasp the concepts. For several years, I carried the *Copyright Law of the United States* around with me. It was a grand source of amusement to everyone. When I went to spin class at Crunch Fitness, I had the Copyright Act book with Post-it notes throughout the pages in my work out bag. My friend Roger still jokes about that. The way I learn is—I teach. I've always been that way—teach, memorize, teach, memorize, teach, memorize.

When I wanted to learn songs for my band, I first taught them to my guitar students. Later, as a lawyer, I taught at the Musicians Institute, which has two-year programs. The degrees were creative degrees like performance, producing, songwriting, and recording. Unfortunately, the students weren't very interested in my music business class. It was the worst part of their day. That's not what they wanted to learn. For an instructor, there's nothing worse than trying to teach kids a subject they don't want to learn about. They just weren't present.

After two years of being there, I transitioned to UCLA Extension, which was awesome! The UCLA campus was a stone's throw away from my office. My class was an extension class, meaning students didn't have to be enrolled as college or law students at UCLA to take it. When I first started teaching the class, people would tell their friends, who would then tell *their* friends, who in turn told *their* friends. Eventually, as my colleagues began running their own companies, they would tell their new employees, "If you really want to understand the business, take Dina's class."

The art of teaching and learning works both ways. As I was teaching students about the complexities of copyright and trademark, they taught me about the culture and internal environments of the record and publishing companies they worked at. This trade-off worked well for me. My clients' managers and agents started sending their employees to my class, and then I'd learn about their management companies and agencies. When some of their new clients needed lawyers, they referred me.

My UCLA class quickly gained recognition. Enrollment also got crazy. Even though we were in the Dodd Hall on campus, I used to cap the class at 100 people because it got to be too much. I enlisted the assistance of some interns and two new lawyers from my firm, Lindsay Arrington and Dominic

Chaklos, to oversee it. I used a headset and microphone while Lindsay walked around the class with a wireless microphone so people could ask questions throughout the class. Many years later, Lindsay and Dominic became partners at the law firm and got married to *each other*.

UCLA was on a quarter system rather than a semester system, and my class always fell in the first quarter. The start date was the first or second week of January, and it ran for twelve weeks to the end of March on Tuesday nights from 7:00 to 10:00 P.M. Enrollment began right after Thanksgiving, and within a couple weeks it reached the 100-person cap. Then I'd have my friends and colleagues calling me saying that their assistants and other associates tried registering but couldn't because the website said enrollment was closed. They'd ask if I could please get them in, so by the time class actually started each year, there were 120 students because I also had the scholarship students from King Drew High School in Compton attending.

By teaching that class for all those years, I got really good at articulating the concepts in the music business and negotiating the deal points in all the agreements, because I understood how they applied. I saw the agreements play out in real time. I also understood the pros and cons of each of the deal points because

I had so many record-industry people from all different areas of the music business in my class. There were managers, accountants, agents, record company and music publishing people, songwriters, and artists. Different people brought different perspectives, too. I also brought in guest speakers—prominent industry people I wanted to meet and learn from as well. It was quite special and exceptionally educational.

It really became impactful for me when I started going down to King Drew High School to award the ten students per a year with a scholarship to my class. These were the students who wanted to be in music but didn't have any connections to get there. It was an enormous commitment for them. Even the KDHS principal had to sign off. The principal had to assess whether each student typically follows through, and if their family is supportive. Many of those students weren't even encouraged to be in high school, let alone schlep all the way to UCLA in Westwood after being at school all day down in South Central Los Angeles.

A lot of those kids were first-generation high school students. The opportunity was there, but they had to take action against a plethora of naysayers. I arranged for a driver and a Sprinter van to pick the students up after school at 2:30 P.M. and drive two hours, in terrible L.A. traffic, to the UCLA campus where I had food waiting for them. They stayed for a three-hour lecture and then went back to Compton. It was usually after 11:00 P.M. or close to midnight by the time they got home, hence the huge commitment. The ones who were really committed to taking the class . . . they were the ones who took action.

In 2016, I once again went against the grain and took a large-scale action. I orchestrated suing the Department of Justice. The government regulates a great deal of copyright through compulsory licensing and government decrees that oversee the nation's two largest performing rights societies, ASCAP (American Society of Composers, Authors and Publishers) and BMI (Broadcast Music, Inc.). ASCAP and BMI collect public performance income for songs that are played on the radio, internet, television and streaming services. The broadcasters, networks, and providers pay ASCAP and BMI, and then ASCAP and BMI pay songwriters and music publishers. Songwriters affiliate themselves with either ASCAP or BMI. It doesn't matter how successful a songwriter is (or isn't), once they sign up, the society must take them.

The other two performance rights societies, Global Music Rights (GMR) and Society of European Stage Authors and Composers (SESAC), only invite big songwriters to join their societies. They won't take just any songwriter; therefore, most songwriters in America are with ASCAP or BMI. In the

1940s, the Department of Justice enacted government decrees over ASCAP and BMI to prevent them from engaging in anti-trust behavior, like extorting vast sums of money from radio stations in exchange for *allowing* them to play the songs they control. Instead, ASCAP and BMI were regulated by these government decrees. These decrees mandated that the royalty rates were, and still are, set by judges in Washington D.C. Now, with all the digital platforms streaming music, the public performance rates for songwriters are extremely low compared to the public performance rates paid to record companies, who are not subject to the government decrees. So, basically, these government decrees are considerably antiquated.

In 2014, ASCAP and BMI convinced the Department of Justice to look at these government decrees for potential updating to keep up with modern times in the digital revolution. This was naïve. Why? Because who would be against this? The radio stations and all the streaming services, that's who. And, trust me, they have a lot more money for lawyers and lobbyists than ASCAP, BMI, and the lowly songwriters. So, ASCAP and BMI went to the Department of Justice in Washington, D.C. to say we need to review and consider updating these government decrees.

In addition to the representatives of music creators like me, the hearings also featured actual songwriters, such as Paul Williams, who wrote "Rainbow Connection" and a bunch of other legendary hits. Their presence aimed to persuade lawmakers of the need for better payment rates and greater flexibility to negotiate in a free market with radio stations and streaming services. Of course, radio broadcasters and streamers went in there as well, with their cadre of well-connected lobbyists, and convinced them otherwise. In fact, they complained that having to pay four different performance rights societies (ASCAP, BMI, GMR, and SESAC) was overkill, and they should just be able to choose to pay ASCAP or BMI, not both. Much to their dismay, GMR and SESAC weren't governed by the government decrees like ASCAP and BMI.

Because of all the lobbying by the radio broadcasters and streaming services, on August 4, 2016, the Department of Justice issued a statement concluding that radio stations and streaming platforms no longer had to pay *both* ASCAP and BMI. Instead, they could choose to pay just one of them. It was then up to those two organizations to figure out how to compensate all songwriters of a song. This was referred to as "full-work licenses." The result was that songwriters would have a significant amount of their income allocated to an organization they weren't even associated with. This was a massive, massive disaster for songwriters, because BMI doesn't have any payment information for the ASCAP songwriters and ASCAP doesn't have any payment information for the BMI songwriters. These are millions and millions of micropayments that, when collected and paid out properly to publishers and songwriters, amount to millions and millions of dollars in public performance income. This puts more onus on the songwriter to try and figure out how to get paid their share of royalties from their co-writers. Songwriters aren't accountants or collection societies. They shouldn't have to deal with all that, which is why they can always affiliate with ASCAP or BMI. Because the Department of Justice couldn't mandate this for GMR or SESAC, secretly, I think both those societies were loving this. After all, the music industry is a cutthroat business.

ASCAP and BMI fought this new, unfair mandate of "full-work licensing." ASCAP wanted to go to Congress and get legislation passed to fix the disaster, while BMI wanted to litigate it. But, per the government decrees, both ASCAP and BMI needed to get "permission" from their rate court judges before they could do anything. For the life of me, I could not see how effective any lawsuit, with watered-down claims that had to first be approved by some rate court judge before it actually is allowed to get filed, would be. Not to mention, I would be 108 years old before Congress actually got anything done, so I decided it was time to take the matter into my own hands. I was already trying to galvanize the songwriting community by educating them on the government decrees and Department of Justice hearings. In fact, months earlier, I had flown to D.C. to meet with the acting attorney general at the DOJ, Renata Hesse, and the other attorneys under her, to explain the plight of songwriters. I told them how horrible it is for songwriters in the music business. The government regulates all their royalties, so they can never really negotiate in a free market. I felt she was empathetic and really understood. But then I thought, "We need to sue this bitch too." She's a hypocrite.

Around the same time, Wendy's cousin, Sarah, who was also sober, was going to recovery meetings with songwriter and recording artist, Kay Hanley. One Saturday, Sarah and her husband Rick were having a barbeque at their house and she told me that she had invited Kay. She asked if Kay could ask me some questions about all these things happening with the songwriters? Immediately, I said yes. I loved Kay Hanley! She was the lead singer of Letters to Cleo and had a hit song, "Here & Now" that I used to play on repeat while I was in law school. A few days later after the barbeque, Kay came to my office with Michelle Lewis, her songwriting partner from their Nickelodeon show who had also been introduced to me by Brendan Okrent at ASCAP. As soon as my reception-ist brought them in, I said, "Where the fuck have you bitches been?!" And for three hours, I educated them on all the government decrees, and what was happen-ing with the DOJ and the hearings. After we finished, they asked if they could come back in a few days with some other songwriter friends. Of course, I said yes.

The next day, Michelle called me and said, "We're going to need a bigger room." Apparently, she and Kay had more than 100 songwriters who wanted to meet with me about the DOJ ASCAP BMI prob-lem. Within days, more and more songwriters were also wanting to join. I called my colleague and fel-low music lawyer, Jay Cooper, and he suggested we reach out to the Recording Academy and ask them to arrange the space. Jay is a legend in the music indus-try. At ninety-six years of age, he is still practicing music law and is as smart as ever. He is such an inspi-ration and is an example of "when you love what you do, it doesn't feel like work." Katy Perry is one of his clients, and he's been her lawyer from the beginning of her career. That's how lucky she is.

Like me, Jay started out as a musician. He was a saxophone player and gigged his way through college and law school by playing with the likes of Frank Sina-tra, Nat King Cole, and Bobby Darin. After law school, he was with the Los Angeles Philharmonic before he left to spend his time practicing law. Back then, there was no such thing as music lawyers, but as he was in the recording studio at night, fellow musicians would ask him if he could look over their recording contracts. He focused on representing the legal interests of musicians and artists, and *voilà*! Music law was a thing!

Jay and I called Daryl Friedman, who at the time was the chief policy officer of the Recording Academy. Daryl ran their advocacy arm in Washington, D.C. Right away, he agreed to rent for us the old Ocean Way Recording studio space in Hollywood, which had a big parking lot and a big wide-open area in the middle of all the recording studios and vocal booths. We held my presentation there.

I had my UCLA students help organize it by making copies of my presentation and checking people in. When everyone was in, it was time for me to explain what the DOJ mandate of full-works licensing actually meant for them. I was so nervous looking out at all the humongous names in the songwriter industry surrounding me! I remember my legs were shaking when I went up on the stage. Among the attendees were people like Holly Knight, who wrote "Love is a Battlefield" for Pat Benatar and co-wrote the Aerosmith smash hit "Rag Doll" with Steven Tyler; Shelly Peiken and Pam Sheyne, who wrote Christina Aguilera's "What a Girl Wants" and "Genie in a Bottle," respectively; and my now client, Siedah Garrett, who co-wrote Michael Jackson's "Man in the Mirror." These were songwriter legends!

At the meeting, Michelle, Kay, and I wanted everyone to sign on so we could be a group. We needed a name. One of the songwriters, Adam Dorn, came up with SONA—Songwriters of North America. More than 200 songwriters signed up! We were officially a group. I found a non-profit lawyer to help us set up a non-profit corporate entity called a 501(c)6, and we were in business! Seven songwriters were initially on the SONA board. Michelle, Kay, Adam Dorn, Shelley Peiken and her husband and fellow songwriter Adam Gorgoni, Pam Sheyne, and producer/songwriter, Jack Kugell.

We needed to file a lawsuit against the Department of Justice, and I explained how ASCAP and BMI had plans to fight it, but that it was going to go nowhere. The SONA board agreed but said ASCAP and BMI were pressuring all songwriters to let them work it out and to *trust them*. I quickly set out to find a litigator who would take our case *pro bono*, meaning, help us for free. I found Gerry Fox, a litigator in Century City. We all met at his office and agreed that suing the DOJ was the way to go. Our principal claim was that songwriters were third-party beneficiaries of the ASCAP and BMI government decrees. This allowed the government to rob them of the right to control their personal property (copyrights) in violation of the Takings Clause of the *Fifth Amendment* in the *United States Constitution*. I thought our argument was magnificent. After all, if you are going to sue the United States government you may as well allege a constitutional violation!

Throughout this process, the lawyers at BMI and ASCAP called and begged me not to do this. They said the songwriters will ruin everything. My response was always, "How much worse can it get?!" A few days before we filed the lawsuit, I had lunch with Jacqueline Charlesworth who was the former General Counsel of the United States Copyright Office. I had met her a few years earlier when I testified at the copyright hearings in Washington, D.C., when they were holding hearings on possible new licensing implementations in the digital age. She had since left the Copyright Office and was buying property in Los Angeles because she wanted to live and practice law in California. I told Jacqueline about our plan to sue the DOJ. She was adamant that I show her a draft of the lawsuit before we filed it and that we allege some administrative claims in addition to the constitutional claims. Ultimately Jacqueline became SONA's co-counsel and redrafted the lawsuit into a genuine masterpiece. Jacqueline was brilliant. We filed it on September 13, 2016. SONA had arrived!

That lawsuit against the Department of Justice put SONA on the map. Starting with Congressman Doug Collins, suddenly all these members of Congress who were on the Judiciary Committee in the House of Representatives were reaching out to us directly, like former Congressman Bob Goodlatte, a prominent Republican from Virginia, and Congressman Jerry Nadler, a prominent Democrat from New York. Congressman Nadler was instrumental in helping to get same-sex marriage passed in the United States, having authored the congressional brief on the Edie Windsor U.S. Supreme Court case in the House and the Senate.

These members of Congress wanted to make sure they had direct contact with the songwriters and their representatives. We emphasized that the publishers and this other big songwriter group in Nashville did not speak for us. The SONA songwriter members were largely in the pop, rock, R&B, rap, and hip-hop field. Although we are quite aligned with the publishers on some things, there are other things we do not align with. It was amazing, because at the end of the day, we got so much credibility with some of these members of Congress and developed some great relationships.

Years later, when we were working on a new songwriter bill, which ended up becoming the *Music Modernization Act*, a piece of legislation that SONA was instrumental in helping get passed in 2018, these members of Congress were already calling us directly. If I hadn't taken action and refused to listen to the people who told us not to sue the Department of Justice, SONA would never have been established, and songwriters would never have had a direct line to members of Congress. If we had listened to the people who told us to wait for ASCAP and BMI to fix it, we would *still* be waiting. We were the renegades! Living in the Wild Wild West. We took matters in our own hands and filed the lawsuit, much to the dismay of everyone who told us not to. I said we needed to take action because we weren't going to sit around and wait for these fucking people to fix our shit.

The other thing I learned is that there are two types of great lawyers. Those with great personalities, who are funny and engaging, and can really read the room. And those who are dry as a bone and have introverted personalities. I set my sights on emulating a great lawyer who had a great personality, was highly ethical, and was very respected. This was Don Passman. He's funny, smart, and engaging, and he's got a great sense of humor.

When you possess all those qualities, you possess magic, and everyone wants to be around you because you come in and control the room. You have a great aura and energy. And if you really understand the laws and the deal points that's the magic sauce and you can be super successful.

Some of my colleagues, although well connected and seem to be successful, don't really know jack shit about the technicalities of copyright and they couldn't articulate a concept if their life depended on it. One thing I used to say to these people when they said, "I want this, and I want that" during negotiations, I would respond with, "If you can explain it to me, you can have it!" That usually would shut them up.

One guarantee: If you don't take action, nothing changes. Nothing! The first thing you have to do is recognize when something isn't going to work. If you're miserable, or if a work situation isn't going well, the first step is to recognize that it's not working. You have to move forward. If you know something needs to happen, and you can identify what needs to happen, you must move forward. Don't listen to other people if they're trying to tell you that you shouldn't be doing that. Fear holds people back, and so does the comfort of relying on other people who say they're going to take care of it. Don't believe other people when they say, "We got this," especially when your intuition tells you they don't.

You have to have the courage to take that first step, regardless of the consequences. Everyone has a natural aversion to feeling uncomfortable when they step out of their comfort zone. People resist uncomfortableness. It puts them in an unknown and unfamiliar space and invites fear to the party. They don't know what's going to happen, so it becomes a matter of realizing that taking action means that doing *something* will change *everything*. You want to change, but you do not want to be uncomfortable. Those things cannot co-exist. You have to get comfortable with being uncomfortable. Take action and be okay with whatever is going to happen. If you stay true to your feelings and actions, you'll get through it.

It's hard to take action when you really don't have a plan. Taking some sort of action is the first step. It doesn't have to be precisely planned out. When Wendy and I first talked about separating, I didn't know what the next step was. All I knew for certain was that we weren't happy together in the house. I had to move out. We didn't have a plan. We had to just let it unfold. I've heard that the universe always has three answers for us: yes; not at this time; or there is something better in store for you.

Nightbirde (Jane Marczewski) was a popular contestant on Season 16 of *America's Got Talent*. She withdrew before the semifinal round because she had Stage IV cancer. She sang her original song, "It's OK" for the judges, which included Simon Cowell. It was so moving that he hit the Golden Buzzer, which sent Nightbirde straight to the live shows. Following her performance, the judges asked about her health and commented on how impressed they were with her voice and the song's lyrics, but also her positivity in light of what she was going through. She said, "You can't wait until life isn't hard anymore before you decide to be happy." Nightbirde's performance went viral after she died.

Taking action isn't always going to be easy, but before you know it, you'll be in the later stages of life. Don't wait. Decide to be happy now.

CHAPTER JOURNAL NOTES

- What is one area in your life where you feel stuck?
- What is one difficult step or decision you have been avoiding?
- Who or what is holding you back from taking action?
- Don't overthink it and get overwhelmed. Make a list of steps. What one thing you can do today to move closer to your goal.
- Look at how you spend your time and energy each day. Is it raising or lowering your vibration.
- Eliminate that which does not align with your end goal. Let go of attachments that don't serve your personal growth and instead embrace any and every little thing that propels you closer to your desired future.

6

Build a Foundation, Not a Fantasy

What is your core foundation? Before venturing into specific areas of expertise, it's important to develop and strengthen your core skill set. If you're all over the map before you establish yourself in your chosen field, you lose credibility, and people will think less of you.

Once you become successful and prominent in your core skill, in whichever career you choose or whatever business you want to build, *then* branch out and do different things because that's when everyone will want your opinion on everything! How do you do this? Education and experience. Unless you're famous, it's rare to build a foundation on just one of these. Ironically, if you are famous then everyone becomes interested in your opinions! The super smart ones like Brooke Shields went back to college and super-smarty Kim Kardashian is taking the bar exam. Pure badasses.

If you're not famous and you have to choose between education or experience, choose experience and the "school of hard knocks," which is much more practical. You can build on that; however, keep in mind that you may eventually hit a wall. Especially if you want to be a lawyer, doctor, accountant, nuclear physicist, or a profession where education *and* experience are required. For example, if you want to become a lawyer, you most often have to go to law school and pass the state bar exam before you can even apply for a license to practice law.

In this era, getting your college degree simply isn't enough. You need experience, and no job is too small. A friend of mine spent years getting her bachelor's degree, two master's degrees, and then her doctorate. It took her thirteen years. Her intention was to open a spiritual center, so that's what she set out to do after finishing her education. Unfortunately, she had no experience outside of her own spiritual journey. If she had dedicated some time to honing a specific skill set, like becoming a pastor, therapist, or even a Reiki Master, her journey toward opening her own spiritual center would have paved a clearer path. She would have earned credibility through her well-established reputation with her congregation or her clients. Reputation is the cornerstone of power, but if you have no reputation, you have no power.

When it comes to being a great example, few can match the achievements and impact of Oprah Winfrey. She was born into poverty in rural Mississippi in 1954. She endured and triumphed over physical and sexual abuse, and faced the challenges of teenage pregnancy, only to suffer the heartbreaking loss of her premature baby boy shortly after his birth. With dreams of being in radio and on television, when she was just nineteen years old, she got her first job as a co-anchor for the local evening news in Nashville where she was going to college.

Oprah stood out as a news anchor. With no preparation and often having only minutes' notice before she was on air, her empathic nature and ability to relay any story with raw emotion set her apart. In 1976, she nabbed an opportunity and moved to Baltimore to co-anchor the six o'clock news. She also started hosting the local version of *Dialing for Dollars*. Building on that reputation, she moved to Chicago to host a morning local TV talk show, *AM Chicago*. Within months of Oprah becoming the show's host, it became one of the highest-rated local talk shows in Chicago, overtaking *The Phil Donahue Show*. *AM Chicago* became nationally syndicated in 1986.

By this time, Oprah had already built a reputation for creating a more intimate and confessional form of media communication. In 1985, she also made her unforgettable film debut playing Sofia in the motion picture, *The Color Purple*, which earned her a Best Actress in a Supporting Role nomination at the Academy Awards.

By the mid-1990s, Oprah had reinvented her show with an emphasis on literature, self-improvement, mindfulness, and spirituality. By the 2000s, *The Oprah Winfrey Show* was one of the most popular talk shows on television. The show boasted mass celebrity appeal, with guests like Julia Roberts, Tom Cruise, Beyoncé, Tina Turner, Jennifer Aniston, Mariah Carey, and even Donald Trump. Her show ran for twenty-five seasons.

Besides her highly successful daytime talk show and acting roles (starring in critically acclaimed films such as *Beloved* in 1998, *The Butler* in 2013, and *Selma* in 2014), she founded Harpo Productions, a film and TV production company. She also started her own television network, *OWN* (the Oprah Winfrey Network). She has also authored several books, ranging from a memoir, *Build the Life You Want*, to a recipe book, *Food, Health, and Happiness: 115 On-Point Recipes for Great Meals and a Better Life.*

She's been called on by multiple politicians, including former presidents Bill Clinton and Barack

Obama, who sought her thoughts and opinions on topics including healthcare, women's rights, LGBTQ+ rights, and social justice reform. There's nothing she can't do, and everyone wants her opinion. All because she built a foundation *first*.

Similarly, Mel Robbins began her career as a criminal defense attorney for Legal Aid in New York City. For years, she made regular guest appearances on CNN as a legal commentator. She later joined CNN as a legal analyst and quickly made a name for herself by extensively covering the George Zimmerman trial in 2013 who was charged with murder in the death of Trayvon Martin.

In 2017, she published her first motivational book, *The 5 Second Rule*, which was named the #1 audiobook in the world. She built an enormous fan base through her social media platforms and went on to host her own daytime TV show for one season, *The Mel Robbins Show*. Her critically acclaimed podcast, *The Mel Robbins Podcast*, has been syndicated in 194 countries and is available in forty-one languages. It consistently averages 1.5 million downloads per week.

Much like Oprah, people across the globe seek her thoughts and opinions on *everything*. Mel Robbins has become one of the most sought-after motivational speakers in the world, and yet she started with a simple core foundation and built on it.

After opening my law firm, I started building my client base and reputation by teaching the music business classes and actively promoting myself by writing articles on music business issues. Teaching the UCLA Extension class was important because I wasn't just teaching college students. I was also teaching college graduates who were already working in the music industry. They took my class to gain a competitive edge.

And as the years went on, my students' roles within the music industry grew more and more influential. As they became more reputable, they began recommending me as a lawyer, and those referrals helped build my client base.

I also started going to music industry conferences like South by Southwest (SXSW) in Austin, Texas; Canadian Music Week in Toronto, Canada; and CMJ in New York City. In addition to learning from the music business panels, I also seized the chance to establish connections with the conference organizers. After attending consistently for a few years, I felt comfortable approaching panel organizers to offer myself as a speaker, specifically on topics like copyright and record deals, which I'd been teaching for years in my UCLA music business class.

I became a frequent speaker on music panels at renowned music industry conferences. That got my name out there in other countries. I found my way to this music-business conference that happened every January in Cannes, France: MIDEM (*Marché International du Disque et de l'Edition Musicale*, which translates to International Market for Recorded Music and Music Publishing). Before the digital revolution, MIDEM held its ground as an important music business conference for more than forty years. In the early days of my career, Afeni Shakur would cover my expenses to attend. I had explained to her the value of me going, especially since we were in the middle of negotiating Tupac's unsettled song copyrights.

After closing a lot of the copyright dispute cases, I went to MIDEM to meet publishers from various countries to ensure they had our newly negotiated copyright splits. These days, you can upload everything into a database but back then I would just print everything and hand-deliver packages to publishing and performance rights executives from France, Germany, Ireland, and South America, among other countries.

I built a lot of relationships that way. These days, most business transactions take place over Zoom, Microsoft Teams, or WhatsApp, but before video conferencing was a thing, industry professionals from every pocket of the world would come together at events like MIDEM. A lot of business and legal panels were about trends and business practices in specific countries, and what each of their market triggers were. And, as you might expect, there was a lot of hanging out, dinners, shows, and partying, too.

While in Cannes, I found the recovery meetings, which were held in a church somewhere off the beaten path, not far from the *Palais de Festivals et des Congrès*. That led to making a lot of sober connections and friends from all over the world.

The amount of experience I've gained is truly remarkable. This was the beginning of building my reputation worldwide. Thanks to the IAEL lawyers' group I joined, I built connections with lawyers in several countries. Ones that I could hire, boots on the ground, to do things for me in their home countries. In return, other IAEL members reach out to me when they need an American entertainment lawyer to help their clients. I've assisted clients in the U.S. who are from and whose lawyers are from India, Germany, Indonesia, Italy, Sweden, and the U.K., so I have a powerful international presence. But to get there, I built my foundation, concentrating on music law in the U.S., and I branched out from there, writing and teaching.

Every year, to coincide with MIDEM, the IAEL lawyers' group released a book highlighting the latest hot topics in the music business. The publication is an amalgamation of articles from the lawyers in the IAEL. The organization elected an editor for the following year, and that editor would then spend the next year developing a book structure and chapter breakdown before soliciting and collecting articles from its members. After years of building connections within the IAEL lawyers' group, submitting articles, and speaking on their panels, I was twice elected to be the editor. The first book, *Building Your Artist's Brand as a Business*, was a big hit at MIDEM.

That year, I organized and arranged the legal panels that featured the lawyers who authored articles for my book. Through this experience, I familiarized myself with the business and legal protocols in different territories across the world and then passed that knowledge along to the students in my UCLA class. The last year I attended MIDEM, I had the privilege of being one of the keynote speakers alongside my friend and client, the legendary record executive, Sylvia Rhone who was responsible for signing or working with some of the biggest and most influential artists in the music industry such as En Vogue, Missy Elliott, Wiz Khalifa, Busta Rhymes, Tracy Chapman, Akon, Lil Wayne, 21 Savage, and Travis Scott, the list goes on and on.

My business has always relied heavily on existing clients, referring their friends who then become new clients. The people in my UCLA class who went on to become big managers, agents, or prominent record and publishing executives also referred clients to my office. Other clients found their way to me from my public speaking engagements at conferences or because they read my published articles. People knew me because my name was out there.

At the onset of social media's rise in popularity, I took the lead in building an online following before anybody in my field. The old-school lawyers who dismissed me in the past didn't even have websites back then. I built mine right away. I developed my firm the non-traditional way because I didn't have anybody to teach or mentor me. I figured it out on my own so people could find me. At first it was through Facebook, and then X (formerly, Twitter), which allowed followers to tweet at me from all over the world or send me direct messages.

By sticking to my core foundation of representing music creators, my reputation grew exponentially. If I got an artist in a particular musical genre, I would expand further in that genre. Having the Tupac estate and working with Afeni Shakur gave me a lot of credibility in the rap and hip-hop community. By the late 2000s, everyone in the rap and hip-hop community knew who I was. And that was massive.

I then branched out into the rock community, being one of the lawyers representing Mötley Crüe, and then I got the legendary Steven Tyler. I also had

Wild Orchid, three girls signed to RCA Records, one of whom later became known as Fergie. When I picked up deadmau5, that catapulted me into the dance and electronic community. That was super interesting in so many ways because deadmau5 isn't only a music artist, but also a technologist who has started and developed multiple platforms. He is still very much ahead of the curve with electronic music. It challenged me intellectually to figure out how to stay ahead of the things he was doing so I could protect his intellectual property. He was making digital pins and playing with cryptocurrency before cryptocurrency was even a thing. It's the same with artificial intelligence. He's been playing around with AI and building games for many years, and people are just now trying to figure out the AI stuff.

Another part of my core foundation as an entertainment attorney was getting involved in public policy. This became one of my unique specialties, and one of the things I became well known for. The best part is that I do it all *pro bono*. It began with Joel Katz, a big music lawyer. Probably one of the biggest ever. One year at MIDEM, I walked into the Carlton Hotel near the convention center and saw Joel sitting alone at a table in the lobby bar, writing on his legal pad. I walked right up to him and said, "Hi, Mr. Katz. My name is Dina LaPolt. I'm a music lawyer and a big fan of yours." He replied, "Oh, you're so nice. Please have a seat and join me for a drink." He told me the person he was supposedly meeting had missed his flight to Nice, and his next meeting wasn't for another hour or so. As we spoke, I was taken aback by his unexpected kindness toward someone like me. He was so gracious with his time.

I wanted to know what advice he would give me if he could only choose one thing. He said to me, "Being in the music industry, we have a unique opportunity because our laws are all federal laws. If you get involved in copyright reform and volunteer to help with some of the music industry copyright initiatives, you get to know a lot of members of Congress and Senators."

In addition to being the head of the entertainment law department of this big-ass law firm, Joel was also the General Counsel of the Recording Academy and was involved in their advocacy arm in Washington, D.C., where he helped oversee their legislative and policy issues. I had watched him make speeches over the years at Grammys on the Hill.

He said there are two forms of power in America: money and influence, and asked if I knew which was more important.

Right away, I answered, "Money, of course."

He replied, "No. Influence is by far more important than money. But, of course, having money always helps." From there, he shared a story that had a profound impact on me and spurred me on another journey, which only served to build my core skill set.

Joel had been representing a big producer and songwriter, Dallas Austin, out of Atlanta. Dallas is known for producing big hits from Madonna, TLC, Michael Jackson, Janet Jackson, and P!nk. In 2006, Dallas went to Dubai to attend Naomi Campbell's birthday party. He was arrested at the Dubai International Airport because he'd been carrying less than a gram of cocaine when he entered the country. Dubai is part of the United Arab Emirates. It's an Islamic country, and its citizens are forbidden from drinking alcohol and taking drugs, in accordance with the Qur'an.

Although the country caters to Western tourists and businesspeople by serving alcohol in lavish hotels, it has strict laws governing illegal drug possession and use. Needless to say, poor Dallas was sentenced to four years in a Dubai prison, but because Joel had a lot of relationships in Washington as a result of all his work in the music law policy space, he called people in the White House, members of Congress, and the Senate to help work out a deal where Dubai ruler Sheikh Mohammed bin Rashid Al Maktoum pardoned him. Dallas got back to the U.S. safely after being held in Dubai for nearly two months. If Joel hadn't been involved in copyright legislation and music industry policy for all those years leading up to Dallas's arrest, he wouldn't have had those political relationships.

As soon as I got back to the U.S. I reached out to a lawyer named Jay Rosenthal. I met Jay a year earlier on a panel at SXSW in Austin. Jay lived in Washington, D.C., and was representing some of the labels and publishers in various copyright hearings. He also was the General Counsel for the then newly formed Recording Artists' Coalition; which was an artist rights group founded by music artists Don Henley of the Eagles, Sheryl Crow, and their manager, Irving Azoff.

Jay Rosenthal became one of my mentors when I began volunteering with him. He just took me under his wing. In 2019, he passed away, but he had been my person, and he taught me so much about copyright reform and policy issues. The best thing about Jay was that he would always meet me at the conferences, whether it was SXSW in Texas, CMJ in New York, or MIDEM in France. He was always there with me. We spoke on panels together. He introduced me to a ton of people, and he had a great sense of humor.

I started writing op-eds on hot-topic issues in the music industry as I was lecturing and speaking about these issues. Over time, I became increasingly recognized in my field as an entertainment lawyer and champion for artist rights. My practice was really taking off, especially after I started representing Steven Tyler. I had the Tupac Shakur estate, Mötley Crüe, and Steven Tyler, and everybody in the industry was trying to take my UCLA class.

The longtime Aerosmith manager, Howard Kaufman, took an instant liking to me. While Steven was on *American Idol* as a judge, the band decided to make a new album and go on tour. I used to go to Howard's house where he'd sit in his big-ass chair taking calls from Europe, booking shows, routing the tour, and teaching me things like how tours are built, what the income participations are, and what you need to look out for with shady promoters. As he taught me all that stuff, he took me under his wing, and I became his person too.

Howard's fabulous wife, Caroline, would make food from scratch when I visited. I asked a ton of questions about his life and career path, as he was a notoriously private person. Before Howard became a manager for rock bands like Aerosmith and Fleetwood Mac, he'd been an accountant in the music industry, and that's how he'd begun building his foundation forty years prior. He developed a great reputation as a business guy and for making his clients a lot of money. Before Howard died in 2017, he taught me a lot about the money and business stuff, but not so much stuff on the legal side.

I took on clients I resonated with, or who resonated with me. Or if they truly needed my services. It was an energy thing. Sometimes an artist or songwriter wanted a new lawyer because their current lawyer had a conflict of interest. Conflicts of interests are rampant in the music and entertainment industry. This means the lawyer (or the law firm) represents the artist, the record company, and/or the publishing company. Sometimes even the manager. For various reasons, artists often stop trusting the record company or manager, and when that happens, it's hard to figure out what side the lawyer is actually on because their law firm represents everyone. Lawyers with conflicts have a fiduciary duty to everyone and can't really piss off one side against the other.

My brand (and my law practice) was built on the principle of not having any conflicts of interest. I started out as an advocate for artists' rights and focused solely on representing music artists and executive talent, not the companies they are signed to or work for. A lot of new executives came from my UCLA class early on, and as they became more prominent, they hired me to negotiate their employment agreements with the company. This became the brand of my firm. Advocacy for artists, songwriters, and the underdog in addition now to representing talent in film and TV and fashion.

One of my greatest referrals came from Tommy Lee, the Mötley Crüe drummer. During the Mötley Crüe: Carnival of Sins tour, the band's tour manager called me late Sunday night, which is never a good sign. That tour was a "circus gone bad" concept with excessive pyrotechnics, unicycle-riding little people, seductive fire-breathing aerialists, and demonic clowns. Tommy Lee's bus was pulled over in Cincinnati, Ohio because he and his best friend, deadmau5, had been drinking excessively and were holding one of the little people from the tour, Mighty Mike Murga, out of the bus and they were driving around a grocery store parking lot. Mighty Mike loved Tommy and deadmau5. All of it could be chalked up to drunken antics, but the cops didn't think it was funny at all.

I got into action and found an attorney in Cincinnati to help mitigate the whole thing. Needless to say, deadmau5 was quite impressed with me. A couple of years later, I met him when he was dating another one of my then-clients, famed tattoo artist Kat Von D, who was on a TV show called *LA Ink*.

deadmau5's career had really taken off, but he was considerably unhappy with how his current lawyer in the U.K. and then business manager were handling things. Kat said, "You should meet with my lawyer," and he replied, "Oh yeah, I know that lady!"

When he came over to my office to meet me, he called Tommy Lee right away to say he'd hired me on the spot. From there, I started growing the electronic and dance music area of my business. deadmau5 had an international presence because electronic and dance music was so popular in Europe. He's also quite clever and had a lot of different businesses that were outside of the U.S., and being from Canada, it was interesting to watch everything unfold. deadmau5 was my first non-U.S.-based client. Although he lived in Canada, he performed internationally and had businesses all over the world. I learned a lot about the international deal-making business because of dead-mau5, and we often connected in person at MIDEM.

While volunteering at the Recording Artists' Coalition, I learned a lot about copyright reform and how it landed on the political spectrum. My first big legislative thing came up in 2012. It started with a call from Steven Tyler. He was upset because paparazzi were pulling their boats up to his property in Maui and using a telescopic lens to look into his house and film him. He told me to "shut them down."

I had a lawyer in my office, Sabrina Ment, find the pictures and publications online before issuing a cease-and-desist letter, just like we do with TMZ

or any other sites or publications based in Los
Angeles. About an hour later, Sabrina came into
my office looking like she'd seen a ghost. She said
the laws in Hawaii aren't the same as in California.
In California, we have laws called the "paparazzi
law," or California Civil Code 1708.8, where a person (or blog) is liable for invasion of privacy when
they knowingly enter onto the land or into the air-
space of another person without permission to capture a visual image of an individual engaging in a
private, personal, or familial activity. For example,
if you're in a California restaurant, huddled in a
cozy booth, there's a reasonable expectation of privacy. If you're in your California living room with
no clothes on, there's a reasonable expectation of
privacy, so someone can't zoom in with a camera
equipped with a telephoto lens and film you. But
in Hawaii, even though the state has privacy protections in its State Constitution, there are no statutory protections, so basically, there was no way
to shut them down. My first thought was, *Oh my
fucking God.*

I called Steven about this and right away we get
into action. I suggest we somehow get in touch with
the governor.

About an hour later, Steven called me back with a
senator on the phone. He said, "Senator, Dina is my

lawyer. Dina, tell the Senator what the laws are in Los Angeles—rather, what they *aren't* in Maui."

He introduced himself as Senator Kalani English, at the time one of the senior members of the Hawaii State Senate, who was first elected in 2001. I informed Senator English about the lack of statutory protection for privacy in Hawaii and discussed the California Civil Code Section 1708.8. Senator English was running for the Senate again and wanted something to talk about for the upcoming election run. He wanted to get ahead of this particular issue and asked me to write up what I thought the law should be for Hawaii. His chief of staff would then look at my draft and make some adjustments.

I'd never written a law before, and Sabrina suggested using the California law as the basis, take out the things we didn't like, add the things we did like, and then send it off to Senator English. It was a great idea, so we did just that, and I sent my draft to him and his chief of staff in December 2012. We titled it the Steven Tyler Act.

The holidays went by and I didn't hear anything. In the middle of January 2013, CNN called my law firm to ask about the Steven Tyler Act. And then we started getting all these Google alerts. Apparently, Senator English's people just took what we wrote and slapped it on the Hawaii State legislature website. I freaked out! I called the senator and asked if there had been some sort of mistake. He assured me there was no mistake and that the draft of the legislation was perfect, so they just submitted it for public comment. I had no idea what that meant.

He explained that when they submit a proposed piece of legislation, the public has time to submit "comment papers" advocating either for or against the proposed legislation. So, when a government body decides that there needs to be a new law or a revision of an existing law, they publish a "call for comments," which means stakeholders (i.e., groups of people who would be affected by that proposed law) follow submission guidelines set forth by the government branch calling for comments.

A committee hearing in Honolulu was scheduled for February 8, and Senator English suggested Steven and I go because there had been a lot of submissions opposing our legislation, including one from the *New York Times*. He told me to be prepared to argue in support of the law in front of the committee. My only thought then was, *"Oh my god, what the fuck have I gotten us into?!?"*

If a proposed piece of legislation passes out of committee, it then goes to the Senate for a vote. I pulled up the link and there were tons of opposition to the Steven Tyler Act, all arguing First Amendment protections. So, there you have it. This country was founded on two main things—freedom of speech and the right to bear arms, so anything that challenges those two topics is basically dead in the water. *Oh, fuck.*

I called Steven and told him what we needed to do. He then called Mick Fleetwood from Fleetwood Mac, who also lived on the island, and the three of us went to the committee hearing together. I contacted Jay Rosenthal, and he helped me get my talking points together. His advice was to print the opposition's comment papers, find out which group was actually coming to the hearing, and prepare my testimony. The *New York Times* was coming, and Jay told me to arrive in Hawaii a few days early to arrange a meeting with some of the committee members. Jay instructed me to get the names of the committee members and then have Senator English introduce them to me a day or two before the hearing. The senator told me there were nine committee members and a lot of them were opposing our bill. Our plan together was to meet as many of them as possible before the hearing.

At the time, I had met this amazing investigator, Jack Struble. He ran background checks on the people my clients wanted to hire, like gardeners, makeup artists, and assistants. Jack did cursory background checks on these committee members so I'd know who

I was dealing with. One of them had two drunk driving incidents. So, when I got to Honolulu and met with that guy, he said, "Steven Tyler can dream on if he thinks I'm going to vote for this."

As this was the fucking drunk guy, I said, "You know, Senator, it's not just for famous people like Steven Tyler, it's for any public figure, like Princess Kekau (who lived on Maui). Under our law, the Princess would be considered a public figure just like you, Senator. If you're around the corner, say . . . at the tavern with other members waiting to be called over for a vote, you should have a reasonable expectation of privacy when you're there. Right now, someone could use a telephoto lens and microphone and eavesdrop on what you're talking about, and there is no recourse."

And just like that, a light bulb went on over his head. I could literally see his energy change. I told him a lot of eyes were on Hawaiian public officials now especially since President Obama had been elected (Obama was from Hawaii). For the first time in the state's history, Hawaiian politicians were under the microscope. They were more famous than ever because of then President Obama.

That meeting resulted in that senator becoming my biggest advocate on the committee. He told some of the other committee members we had his full support and then they also got on board. After Steven, Mick, and I testified at the hearing, we passed the bill out of the committee, and it was all over the internet by the end of the day! Our bill also went to the Senate floor that same day. They even asked Steven to lead the Senate in the opening prayer. And he did. They passed the bill, 31–1. Wow! It was an amazing feat. What a high! Months later, we found out our bill didn't pass in the Hawaii House of Representatives, but some parts of it were added into other pieces of legislation. That's how it all works. Whatever dude.

About a year later, my first big copyright situation came up. Since I began volunteering for the Recording Artists' Coalition, Jay Rosenthal had been telling Irving Azoff about me, and I finally got to meet him. Besides managing the Eagles and Sheryl Crow, he had other big acts like Gwen Stefani and No Doubt. He'd read about our Hawaii legislative hearing in *Billboard*.

Irving asked if I knew what was happening with the anti-copyright initiative coming out of the Patent and Trademark Office. It was very weird because the Patent and Trademark Office sits in the commerce department and regulates just what you'd think— patents and trademarks, not copyrights. Whereas, the United States Copyright Office oversees copyright and sits in the Library of Congress. Two very separate and very different branches of government.

Apparently, this initiative seemed to be trying to take some of the music creators' rights away. I immediately got involved. Boots on the ground! I quickly found out what was really happening—a slew of academics were rallying to change something in the copyright act. Professor Peter Menell of Berkeley School of Law, located just outside of San Francisco in the ultra-liberal city of Berkeley, was behind the movement. One thing I learned is that a lot of liberal academics (and Democrats), like Professor Menell, are against copyright because they want such material to be available for free. "Well, this is not good," I thought. As an openly gay woman, siding on anything with the Republicans was uncomfortable, to say the least but Irving had put some Republican politicians in touch with me because they were looking for constituents to get involved.

Republicans generally prefer that copyright and intellectual property owners negotiate in a free market *without any* government regulations. In contrast, the liberals want to make it all available for free, which may mean tons of government regulation and compulsory licensing.

Professor Menell was advocating for a proposed revision to copyright law that would take away the rights of copyright holders and music creators to deny the use of their music in commercials, films, television shows, action games, samples, and remixes. This specific right under the Copyright Act is referred to as a *derivative use*, and creators are very particular about derivative uses. Although non-commercial remixes (i.e. playing the songs out in a club) are generally industry custom and accepted in the dance and electronic music scene, selling those remixes for commercial gain without written permission is not. This is literally the only section of the Copyright Act that allows copyright holders and music creators to negotiate in a free market or deny the use of their music altogether. For songwriters this is huge because all other uses of their songs are regulated by the government and subject to compulsory licensing. And compulsory means to compel, so it's not a voluntary negotiation.

So, this copyleft law professor was spearheading an initiative within the Patent and Trademark Office to create a compulsory license in a remix which had the whole music industry up in arms. He probably went to the USPTO because if he tried doing it with the Copyright Office, they'd have booted him out on his ass.

Apparently, a lot of his students were remixing music as deejays in the clubs, but the minute they tried to sell the music on CDs or the streaming services, they faced lawsuits. Professor Copyleft decided to "represent the people" and lobby Washington,

D.C. to create a compulsory license for this derivative work. What an ass.

Jay Rosenthal suggested I write a comment paper opposing this. Ha! It was Hawaii and our Steven Tyler Act all over again, but this time I was on the other side. I called Steven, who is very particular about the use of his music, and we submitted the comment paper together, right off the heels of our big win in the Hawaii State Senate. I started working on our comment paper during the 2014 Super Bowl weekend. Jay let Irving know what I was doing, and then Irving told me he'd help get letters of support. I thought, *"Wow! We're gonna hit a home run!"* I whipped up a draft letter of support for Jay's review, and then Irving and Steven sent it to potential supporters. Almost instantly, we received signed copies from Don Henley, Mick Fleetwood, Ozzy Osbourne, and the Chicks (formerly the Dixie Chicks), among others.

My friend, Ann Chaitovitz, was part of the copyright task force at the Patent and Trademark Office, and I let her know how excited Steven and I were to be doing what we were doing. The fact that the USPTO was sticking its nose in copyright affairs caused quite a controversy in the world of music public policy. A few hours after I contacted Ann, she called me back to tell me I missed the deadline. I said, "What deadline?" Comment papers were due three days ago on February 6. It was February 9, so Ann couldn't take mine. I shrugged it off, thinking, *Who cares? I'm almost done.*

I told Ann that we need to try and get her boss on the phone. These were big music artists I was dealing with. There had to be a way around submitting a comment paper after the deadline. She told me it would be difficult to get her boss, Shira Perlmutter, on the phone because it was Sunday, and that it would have to wait until Monday morning. Furious, I called Shirley Halperin who, at the time was a journalist and editor at *Billboard* magazine and a good friend of mine, to ask if she wanted to write about our amazing comment paper. If the stupid trademark office didn't want to know what Steven Tyler thought about people remixing his songs without permission, at least the entire world would.

The next morning, Ann called asked if I was available to talk to Shira. I said to put her on, but it apparently didn't work that way. Ann first had to find out what time *she* was available to talk to me. *Billboard* was running the story anyway, so soon everyone would know what was going on. Within a half hour, I was on the phone with Shira.

In a flat, politically correct tone, she said, "I thank you so much for your interest in copyright. I'm really, really, really honored that you and Mr. Tyler are taking this interest, and it's no wonder you have thoughts about this issue, and that's important. And I'm just giving you so many accolades for that; however, the deadline has passed, so we really can't accept submissions or any other comment papers. It was a very public deadline but thank you. Please be on the lookout for any hearings on the issue. We'd love to hear your thoughts at that time. I thank you again for your interest."

I responded, "Wait a second. We never saw any public deadlines for this stuff. Was it in *Billboard* or *Rolling Stone*?"

Shira said the notice had been posted on the patent and trademark office website and also in the Federal Register. Huh?

I didn't even know what that was, so I said, "Okay, so you don't want to know what Steven Tyler thinks about copyright and remixing songs? No problem! *Billboard* is very interested in his opinion, and they'll be publishing it for us." I thanked Shira for her time and hung up. Less than an hour later, Shira called me back to say she was graciously making an "unprecedented exception" for Steven. She'd accept our late submission, so we didn't have to make a big fuss by letting *Billboard* run the story. That was great!

I uploaded our comment paper to the USPTO's website for Shira and may have neglected to mention that *Billboard* was already running the story that night, regardless. It created quite a ruckus. A lot of artists and songwriters read the article, and it pissed them off that this was happening. They called, emailed, and tweeted, and we ended up killing that initiative. That was my first real foray into copyright policy stuff, and it became a big part of my foundation. In the music business, having respect and credibility in copyright circles in Washington, D.C. is crucial.

With policy, those two things happened: The Steven Tyler Act in Hawaii, and the proposed compulsory licensing of remixes and samples. Both were right in the public eye. It made the record companies and publishers crazy. Until that time, or until the establishment of the Recording Artists' Coalition, the only people fighting for artists' rights in Washington were the trade organizations that represented record labels or publishers. Except for the Nashville Songwriters Association International (NSAI) and the Recording Artists' Coalition, there were no other prominent creator led advocacy organizations to do so. As more and more politicians were getting to know me, they would contact me for input when the record labels were lobbying them. They'd say to one another, "Let's get a good pulse for this and check with Dina."

I'm an advocate for music creators and other talent. It's my core foundation. People consult with me because I know the value of getting along with people to build relationships and foster a connection without "over-lawyering" or being a total asshole. I started building relationships with the people who ran the industry trade organizations or represented either labels or publishers. At first, they weren't necessarily appreciative of me getting all up in their business, but eventually they learned to appreciate what I brought to the table. We became a team and worked together for the betterment of the music industry.

Until I came along, there wasn't anyone like that except for Joel Katz, who acted as the General Counsel of the Recording Academy, but he was getting paid a shit ton of money and everyone knew it. Joel was well known in the policy space. They had lobbyists working at their national law firm, Greenberg Traurig, but I was just little Dina in my little law practice, not getting paid a dime. Just fighting for what's right. As I got to know these politicians, I emphasized that I don't represent anybody but music creators. I would also mention that I pay my own way to come to Washington to talk to them.

They usually would ask about someone who came to see them if they didn't know them already. I'd clarify things like . . . that lawyer represents Sony Music, or that one represents Universal, and that guy is paid by such-and-such law firm. They called me to check on shit, and I'd educate them. The labels and publishers resented the fact that they had to get me on board. And they still do this.

I had some behind-the-scenes involvement with establishing some guardrails surrounding the use of artificial intelligence with music artists and record labels. My friend and colleague, Susan Genco, who works for Irving Azoff and is on the board of the Music Artists' Coalition, originally she got our creator groups involved with these efforts led by SAG-AFTRA, the actors' and musicians' union. She led the charge on our behalf. Although the musicians' union doesn't get involved in record deal negotiations with artists, some of their collective bargaining portions of recording agreements (on behalf of session musicians) still seek to create industry precedent. So we always use the opportunity to involve them because they have bad ass paid lobbyists. We have three music-creator advocacy organizations now that work together in tandem. Besides the Songwriters of North America (SONA), we have the Black Music Action Coalition (BMAC) and the Music Artists' Coalition (MAC), which is just a new and better version of the Recording Artists' Coalition. Our organizations are three of the music creator rights groups behind the scenes.

I usually learn about issues through artists or lobbyists. Occasionally, I figure out that certain issues need my personal attention. For example, this whole business of using lyrics of songs against people as evidence of their guilt—only happens to Black people. I found out about this issue in December 2020 when Shirley Halperin (who had left Billboard and who was now working for *Variety* magazine) asked if I'd read a recent court of appeals decision from the State of Maryland. The prevailing law in Maryland was that they could use rap lyrics to convict people.

"*This is so racist!*" Shirley had said.

I was horrified after reading the decision. This guy in Maryland was convicted solely on the use of his rap lyrics. No other evidence linked him to the crime, and he was sentenced to prison!

Shirley asked if I wanted to write an editorial for *Variety*, so I did. It was published in January 2021, and people from all over the country contacted me: artist managers, professors, criminal defense lawyers, legislators. They all wanted to know what we could do to stop this from happening, so I teamed up with Willie "Prophet' Stiggers, the head of BMAC, and we put together a rap music legislative working group. I then turned that memo I wrote for Congresswoman Zoe Lofgren during the 21 Savage incident into a "white paper," which is basically a memo that outlines an issue for potential legislation.

Jack Lerner became part of the working group. He was a professor at the UC Irvine School of Law where he also ran a law clinic. He'd spent years creating a legal treatise on this very issue called *RAP on Trial: A Legal Treatise for Criminal Defense Attorneys.* Professor Lerner and his law students had already done all the social science research on this issue, which he presented to our working group. His research showed that in the United States, over 500 Black men were sitting in prison because they'd been convicted solely on the use of their lyrics. This phenomenon was exclusive to rap and hip-hop, a genre dominated by Black artists.

After we turned the 21 Savage memo into a congressional legislative white paper, I prepared an exhibit featuring a list of well-known (and violent!) country songs. Those artists were never charged with jack shit. Professor Lerner explained that published studies have taken a song and given it to different artists across various musical genres—such as rock, country, pop, R&B, and rap—to record. The researchers then divide a study group into smaller groups, with each group listening to one version of the recorded song. In every instance where the rapper performed the song, it evoked feelings of fear among the listeners.

Once we finished the legislative memo, I reached out to Congressman Hank Johnson, who at the time was the chair of the Intellectual Property Subcommittee in the House. He agreed to be the primary sponsor of the bill in Congress to ensure that what happened in Maryland would never be repeated with the implementation of a federal law. Prophet also reached out to then-Congressman Jamaal Bowman of New York. Congressman Bowman became the co-sponsor. Prophet and I got help from Harvey Mason Jr. and the Recording Academy, too.

We all worked to put together the *Restoring Artistic Protection Act*, otherwise known as the *Rap Act*, which was introduced to Congress in 2022. Right away, it got a lot of opposition, especially from the Republicans, of course, so we had to spin it to make it about free-dom of speech, otherwise we would have fuck all for Republican support. We had trouble getting a major-ity of support for it in Congress, so our group started focusing on states' rights. Phil Wolosky, a prominent D.C. lobbyist set out to run strategy on all of it.

The first state to get a bill passed was California. California Representative Reggie Sawyer-Jones spon-sored the *Decriminalizing Artistic Expression Act*. Prophet and I helped rally artists to join a Zoom meeting with California Governor Gavin Newsom when he signed it. It was an incredibly special occasion. Phil led the charge to get a bill passed in Louisiana, making it all about freedom of speech, so it got a lot of Republican support and actually passed. Now we have a coalition called Free Our Art which includes our three creator groups, the Recording Academy, SAG-AFTRA, RIAA and many others. We have active bills in Georgia, Missouri, and New York.

This experience all goes back to building a foundation. Once you build a core foundation, you can keep building on it. I started my own law firm and spent years learning about copyright law and concentrating on representing only music creators, which led to an opportunity to teach what I knew about it at UCLA Extension. Those experiences led to volunteering for an artists' rights advocacy organization and meeting copyright policy lawyer, Jay Rosenthal, who suggested going to Washington, D.C. to lobby with some of my artists. That led to meeting a bunch of politicians, which led to the creation of Songwriters of North America.

Had I not established those political relationships, 21 Savage probably would have been deported, separated from his three small children and the rest of his family. It's all interrelated and goes back to what Joel Katz told me at MIDEM: "There are two forms of power in America—money and influence, and influence is by far more powerful."

CHAPTER JOURNAL NOTES

- What skills make up your current foundation?
- How can you expand and strengthen them through practical experience and/or further education if needed?
- Don't be discouraged about where you think you are. Take small steps to help you grow in your area of expertise.
- Focus your efforts on tasks that play to your strengths. Do you know what they are? How can you develop them further?
- Once your strengths are stable and focused, you will grow. Your base will be solid and genuine, not a fantasy playing in your imagination.

7

Mad Men Realty vs. Barbie World Fantasy

Here's a jarring thought: *It's a man's world.* Actually, it's a *white, straight* man's world. Every president of the United States has been a man. Most CEOs and chairpersons of boards of directors are men, and so are most billionaires.

As of 2023 in the U.S., the number of women holding the prestigious role of CEO within Fortune 500 companies stood at a modest fifty-two. To put this limited representation into perspective, women make up a mere 10.4 percent of CEOs of Fortune 500 companies. Out of the top fifty Fortune 500 companies, thirty-seven of the CEO positions are held solely by white men. In stark contrast, only seven of the CEO positions in the top fifty companies belong to women. How great would it be for society if the statistics were flipped?

In 2023, a movie that Greta Gerwig wrote and directed called *Barbie* was released. It is a live-action film based on Mattel's Barbie dolls. The movie starts off in "Barbieland," which is a quintessential matriarchal society completely run by women. The Barbies demonstrate societal roles, showcasing careers like doctors, lawyers, judges, physicists, pilots, and more. The president of Barbieland, played by Issa Rae, is a Black woman. The men in this society play an obsolete role and their job is to "beach," which is essentially sitting and looking pretty. By a strange turn of events, Barbie, played by Margot Robbie, must venture out to the "real world" to solve a crisis in Barbieland. To her dismay, when Barbie enters the real world, she discovers the cruel reality that a patriarchal, sexist, and misogynistic society exists beyond her world. Everywhere Barbie ventures, she sees that men hold all positions of power while simultaneously degrading and putting women down. Not too different from how I grew up.

Women rule Barbieland, and they all have positions of power and maintain the classic Barbie look, but *Mad Men* is the reality. Women still need to look like a Barbie in a *Mad Men* world, because Barbie's world, where women are in charge of everything, is still a fantasy. To be really successful in a corporate business environment, women still have to be put together like Barbie.

As women age, they're judged harshly for it. The older you get, the more you have to be put together. When I was in my early thirties, I wore hardly any makeup when I went to the office. Most mornings, I came right from my recovery meetings or a workout class at the gym. But now I'm in my late fifties. I have to be more put together. In the later years, you become more conscious of how people relate to you. How they perceive you is still important, especially in this day and age. You don't want to be written off just because of age or what you look like. Sadly, us women are still dealing with that.

There are things we can do to change the male-dominated landscape, like engaging in activism and policy or effecting real change by creating awareness and changing and/or making laws. But here is a startling fact—the Equal Rights Amendment (ERA) was proposed in 1923 and finally passed in Congress in 1972 but was never ratified into the Constitution. Under U.S. law, amendments to the Constitution must be ratified by three-fourths of the Senate and then the archivist of the United States (appointed by the president) must formally publish the amendment for it to be ratified. As of this writing, that has not happened. The ERA would guarantee women equal pay and legal rights. On April 27, 2023, a *full* century after its introduction, the U.S. Senate *again* failed to ratify the ERA by a vote of 51–47. It required sixty votes to pass. Truth be told, since the U.S. Supreme Court overturned *Roe v. Wade* in 2022, which decriminalized abortion nationwide and recognized a woman's right to choose whether to have an abortion, the situation for women's rights in the U.S. is the worst it's been in over half a century. We are going backwards!

In the meantime, acceptance of this reality is the only way to turn lemons into lemonade. As they say in the rooms of recovery: *God, grant me the serenity to accept the things I cannot change, the courage to change the things I can, and the wisdom to know the difference.* As we seek to make change for ourselves, we must adapt if we are to rise, grow, and be successful within our current reality. So, if you want to be at the top of your game, learn how to *play* the game, the "man game."

Most men love beautiful and stylish women, even gay men. *Work it!* Whether you're a young business executive at a company or a creative person working in an art gallery, learn how to work within the Mad Men reality and move the needle for yourself. How do you do this? Through various means, like having a magnanimous personality and being able to "work the room," but which only comes naturally to some people.

Women can control and manipulate some things, such as self-care and practicing wellness. Other than the traditional forms of health and wellness like fitness, nutrition, preventive doctor's visits, and getting eight hours of sleep each night (which are all important) women also have more new and improved modern forms of self-care: fashion, medicine, surgery, and also through restoring and improving facial balance and harmony though "natural intention beauty guidance" as described by Medical Aesthetic Providers Vanessa Lee and Christine Son at The Things We Do. These procedures include Botox, hyaluronic acid fillers, biostimulatory fillers, microneedling, blood boosters, and other injectables that stimulate collagen production in the skin. There's a framed picture of Coco Chanel hanging in my plastic surgeon's office in Beverly Hills with one of her famous quotes: *Nature gives you the face you have at twenty; it's up to you to merit the face you have at fifty.* She also said, "A girl must be two things: classy and fabulous." Bottom line: if women are to be successful in a man's world, they must take control of their *physical* appearance as well as their emotional and mental health.

It's not 1970 anymore. Women have access to a wealth of tools to enhance their beauty. We are not our mothers or grandmothers. As a woman in business, what I've learned is—when you *look* good, you *feel* good! And when you *feel good*, you radiate confidence. And guess what? A woman who looks great and radiates confidence can a run a meeting full of men! In my experience, the better you look, the dumber the men become, and then you can sweep the room with your ideas or business proposals.

Even with genetic or hormonal challenges, women can discover ways to improve how they feel. Doctor-prescribed medication can treat most things like mood disorders, obsessive-compulsive disorder, depression, anxiety, bipolar disorder, and hormone irregularity. Women of all ages go through periods of low hormones and should have a doctor who specializes in women's health (obstetrics and gynecology) to check hormone levels regularly. The three hormones are testosterone, estrogen, and progesterone. News flash: women need a balanced combination of all three to function at optimum levels.

Many of today's young women suffer from polycystic ovary syndrome or PCOS, which is a hormone imbalance. PCOS is the most common endocrine disorder in women of reproductive age. Low hormones can cause fertility issues, irregular menstrual cycles, low energy, bloating, unwanted weight gain, depression, anxiety, hot flashes, night sweats, trouble sleeping, vaginal dryness, low sex drive, tender breasts, migraines, thinning hair, and dry skin. Women *cannot* afford to suffer any of this, especially when trying to be a power bitch. For me personally, I am on all three hormones now, in addition to a low dose of metformin, which prevents weight gain after menopause. Thanks to modern medicine, FDA-approved and physician prescribed drugs like Wegovy, Ozempic, Rybelsus, and Mounjaro can also be used to treat unwanted weight gain.

Society's standards for aging are very different for men. The double standard of aging insists that appearance standards are higher and narrower for women. For women, beauty is largely equated with youth, whereas men have more diverse options. While aging is often associated with a loss of visual and sexual allure for women, older men may be considered sexy and handsome. Men tend to maintain a more youthful appearance longer than women. This is because men lose collagen—a protein in the skin that keeps it hydrated and elastic—more gradually than women. Society perceives the loss of youthful looks for women as detrimental, and age discrimination is rampant against them. Basically because Congress did not ratify the ERA, ageism remains legal. Some states, like New York and California, have more protective laws than others, but it's still a shit show

Besides preventative medicine (i.e., going to the doctor regularly and having consistent check ups, screenings, etc) and getting sober, my wellness routine consists of going to recovery meetings, working out, eating the right foods for my body, meditation, Reiki, medications, surgeries, and other beauty guided services like facials, botox, fillers, microneedling, blood boosters, and Sculptura. Since age thirty-eight, my plastic surgeries have included liposuction, an eyelid lift, skin removal surgery around my waist, Lasik eye surgery, and a boob job. My workout routine now consists of weight training four times a week (which is very important for women over fifty) in addition to walking on my treadmill, riding my indoor Peloton bike, or going to a cycle class so I get some cardio in. I also love yoga. At my age, weight training is much more important than a ton of cardio. With age, I came to understand that our physical attributes are somewhat predetermined, but we have the power to alter them. I learned this important lesson thanks to Chaz Bono.

Chaz is the only child of Sonny and Cher. I met Chaz in my recovery group and one day during our recovery step practice, Chaz springs on us that he was filing a name and gender change with the city on Monday because he was transitioning from female to male. I thought to myself, *You're the only child of Sonny and Cher. You don't just go and transition your name and gender on a Monday. This has to be orchestrated.*

In any case, I represented Chaz, and his gender transition was planned and coordinated with the help of attorney Kristina Wertz from the Transgender Law Center in San Francisco. We chronicled the entire process in a documentary called *Becoming Chaz*, directed by Randy Barbato and Fenton Bailey, and produced by their company, World of Wonder. Everyone in his family participated in it, and it was truly lovely.

Years after Chaz transitioned, his late publicist, Howard Bragman, and his former manager, Susan Haber, booked him on *The Doctors*, a popular daytime television show, where he appeared before and after his significant weight loss. Chaz, Howard, and I arrived on set and were directed to the green room to wait for our segment. The show's resident plastic surgeon was Dr. Andrew Orton, who is well known for his work in Beverly Hills. While we were waiting, Dr. Orton came into the green room to see Chaz. Just then, there was a power outage in the studio, and filming stopped until the power was restored, which took about half an hour.

Chaz and Dr. Orton did wonderfully on their segment. As we were leaving, Dr. Orton gave me a big hug and said, "It was such a pleasure to meet you," as he squeezed the excess fat around my back and waist that spilled over my pants. He then added, "You should come see me."

In my head I was like, *Fuck you!* I was so pissed. Of course, I didn't say that to him, but I was insulted. As

I drove Chaz home, I complained about how rude Dr. Orton had been. Chaz simply said, "I don't know why you're upset. He's just trying to help you. You should go see him. It's next to impossible to get in with him." And blah blah blah. Chaz. Typical guy.

With Chaz's insistence, I went to see Dr. Orton and his partner, Dr. Ritu Chopra. I took off my clothes and told them about my workout routine, which was comprised of seven Soul Cycle spin classes per week. Dr. Orton said, "No matter how many spin classes you do, this is never gonna go away." As he grabbed what I thought was my side and back fat, he followed up with, "This is skin. The only way to prevent it from hanging over your pants is to get rid of it. This is our specialty—we eliminate excess skin. I can offer you a significant discount. Trust me, this will be the best thing you'll ever do." And I did it. And it was one of the best things I've ever done.

Fashion is a big part of my business, and music artists and fashion-forward celebrities set the fashion trends around the world. You can't go to a meeting with Cardi B or Steven Tyler and look like a *slob kabob*, as my friend and celebrity manager, Alexis Fisher would say. As an entertainment attorney, I'm constantly in meetings with high-profile people. I typically opt for a suit. A trendy *fitted* suit. Most women make the mistake of buying a suit, dress, or jacket and wear it right off the rack. For women, that is a *big* mistake.

A simple hem, tuck, or dart under each breast can make you look like a million bucks! Don't be fooled into thinking you need to spend thousands and thousands of dollars on high-fashion brands. As you become more and more successful, your wardrobe will naturally evolve and expand. When starting out, if you have to choose between buying a luxury brand like Gucci or investing in high-quality unbranded clothing and having those pieces fitted, do the latter. Trust me, once you have your outfit tailored, it'll look like you're wearing a name brand. You can readily find a local tailor online, or most dry cleaners have someone on staff who can help.

Part of my value in the music industry policy space is getting high-profile music creators to advocate for our legislative measures and/or introducing them to influential members of congress or the senate. Washington, D.C. is by no means the fashion capital, and dark blue and gray seem to be the predominant colors there. I have a myriad of blue, gray, and other muted-tone suits in my closet specifically for my trips to Washington, D.C. None of them are name brands, but they're all *fitted*, and I look like a million bucks! I can tell you that at least one woman in D.C. has gotten the memo, though. Prior to being elected

Vice President of the United States, then-Senator Kamala Harris represented our great state of California. Every time I brought an artist or songwriter to visit her, she looked like a million bucks! Besides being drop-dead gorgeous, she was always wearing a fitted suit. It's fashion's unspoken secret.

The ratio in my firm is 80–20 in favor of women. I hire mostly women. I love strong women. The two men at the firm are my partners Dominic Chaklos and Tom Dean, who are great with strong women. That's why they're there. Both of them married strong women. That's how great they are.

Many of the resumes being sent around the industry are from white men, so I really have to be intentional about hiring women and people of color. It takes time and patience. With a multitude of incredible and unique traits, like resilience, compassion, intuition, and adaptability, women make great multitaskers. They can handle it all, read a room, and then figure it out. My goal is to offer women unique opportunities they might not find elsewhere. I don't think any other law firm of our stature empowers women as much as we do.

With that being said, women really have to set their intentions. Be 100 percent committed and go the extra mile. Adopt the mantra, *failure is not an option*. It's not like that for men. In most industries (and certainly

DINA LaPOLT | 177

in entertainment), opportunities are skewed towards men. Not so much towards women or people of color. Women and people of color need to be hyper-focused and determined, and *create* opportunities for themselves. No one is going to do it for you.

While Harvard Law School doesn't offer many scholarships, it does provide some need-based aid, which is awarded mostly to people of color. The catch lies in a policy that requires recipients who secure summer internships to turn most of their earnings over to Harvard. So, once you get an internship, which is hard enough as it is, you have to turn the first $9,500 you make over to Harvard. Who the hell can afford to do that? Rich white people, that's who. Ridiculous.

I was hoping to hire this brilliant Black woman from Harvard Law School for the summer. Susan Genco, who still teaches an entertainment law class at UCLA, referred this woman to me. I loved her and offered to hire her. That's when the reality of the Harvard policy really sunk in. If she took the internship, she wouldn't have been able to afford to pay rent or buy groceries if nearly all her earnings had to be turned over to Harvard. A lot of privileged white people don't have those issues.

While teaching at UCLA, I had everyone in the class introduce themselves and share why they enrolled. Each person had a turn with the microphone. The variety of introductions was quite enlightening. When a white guy was up, he'd say something like, "Yeah, my name's Jim. I got no experience and moved here from Albuquerque, but I'm gonna run a big record company and make a million bucks. I'm gonna be the biggest executive in the world, and I'm here to kill it." When a woman took the microphone, in a real meek, mousy voice, she'd say, "Hi, I'm Denise. I drove all the way from New York to take your class and I'm really excited to be here. I was elected president of the entertainment law society at my college, and I'm studying copyright law and taking a class online so I can really understand it. And hopefully, hopefully, I will end up being a music lawyer at a great firm." Next, a person of color takes the microphone, and it's just: "Hi, I'm Jerome." Pass the mic. That's it.

With more than one hundred people in my class, there's a flood of information by the end. To sum it up, every white guy has no experience but is going to be a multimillionaire and will run everything. Every woman is super fucking prepared, super fucking educated, has experience, but is just *hoping* for an opportunity to get her foot in the door. Meanwhile, none of the people of color revealed anything about themselves. And that's where we were at.

I would say to the students: "We need to change the gender and race dynamics in this class." I made it a point to engage with the women and people of color who seldom raised their hands. By speaking directly to them, I aimed to establish a personal connection and create a safe environment where they could feel comfortable opening up about their career aspirations and desires. I dedicated years to this effort to create opportunities for them.

In 2021, when we were hiring a film and TV lawyer, most applicants were men. And here I thought the music industry was bad. The film and TV industry—holy shit! It took over a year to find a suitable candidate. When hiring people, you have to be really intentional with addressing the gender imbalance or increasing diversity especially now that the political climate in America is clawing back on diversity, equity, and inclusion. Ultimately, we needed to find the right fit for our firm's culture. Someone with the right mindset. None of the male applicants had as much experience as the woman we hired but they all wanted more money and come in at a senior partner level above all other partners who had been with me for years.

When I was in law school and playing in my lipstick lesbian band, we played a residency every third Saturday of the month at JR's Night Club, a gay nightclub in town. We'd also play different gay pride events in the summer. At a pride event in Salt Lake City, I had some time to kill and bought the *Billboard* magazine that had caught my eye. It was the "Top Music Lawyer" issue. This was the mid-nineties. While flipping through it, I checked out the music lawyers at the record companies, publishing companies, law firms—and it was a lot of fucking men. However, there was a picture of a firm, Guido, Codikow, and Carroll. The picture was of two guys and a woman! This law firm was on the list. SHE was on the list! The fucking woman. I put a Post-it on that page, and I must have carried that magazine around with me for ten years. Her name was Rosemary Carroll.

It wasn't until years later, after I established myself as a lawyer and had my own successful firm, that I got to meet Rosemary. She was based in New York City but had bought a house in New Paltz where I grew up! When I discovered this, I reached out via email, and to my surprise, she replied, saying she knew of me. We met in New Paltz, where I shared my story with her. By the end of our conversation, she was genuinely moved.

Rosemary's firm had an office in Los Angeles, and during one of her visits to the city, she stopped by my office. Everyone knew she was coming, and the excitement was palpable. I announced, "This is Rosemary Carroll!" The reaction was overwhelming—everyone was in awe. It was an emotional moment, and I could see tears in her eyes. Back then, she was the only female lawyer featured on that list. What a true legend!

It's tough for women to make it in the entertainment business. In music, all three major record companies are run by white, straight men, as are most movie studios and streamers. If you look like you don't take care of yourself, you won't reach your full potential. We work in a superficial, cutthroat motherfucking industry, and that's the reality.

Men often stroll into the office or show up for lunch meetings in hoodies or T-shirts and sneakers. Women can't do that unless they are famous or already a very prominent person in the industry and even then, there is judgment. Women must always be put together. This is how you stay in the room. Getting into the room is one obstacle to overcome, but then staying in the room is a completely other obstacle.

This is just the reality of the business. These are tips for succeeding in a man's world. Take care of yourself and *always* put yourself together to look like a million bucks. When you take care of yourself, you feel good; and when you feel good, you look good, and that gives you strength and confidence. It's all interconnected.

CHAPTER JOURNAL NOTES

- What can you do for yourself to build confidence without a big budget? Eliminate alcohol and/or sugar? Start walking every day? Join a gym? Take a yoga class?

- Look at your wardrobe. Are you holding on to things that don't look good on you? Get rid of everything that doesn't make you look or feel great.

- Find a tailor (even at a local dry cleaner) and have your business clothes tailored to a perfect fit, then admire the improved look in the mirror. See a difference?

- Once your budget starts growing, find an aesthetician. Make regular appointments.

- Invest in feeding your self-esteem. Grow your confidence. Walk and carry yourself as though you belong in this world . . .

- . . . Because you do!

8

Preparation and Negotiation

No matter what industry, women who want to compete and win in business must be prepared. Often, women need to be *over*-prepared especially in meetings. What is the meeting about? Who will be in the room or on the Zoom? Who will lead the meeting? Will I be expected to speak on an issue, or am I just listening in? If someone in the meeting pivots to me unexpectedly, am I prepared to respond?

You must think about all these questions before walking in or logging on.

If business is the arena you're playing in and intending to win, it's not optional. Many times, I've found myself in boardrooms or negotiations where I was the sole female presence. To win men over or get what you want for your client, you must be super-prepared. I've seen big male executives sit there, not really knowing what's going on or what the issues are, often relying on their employees or colleagues to brief them right then and there! Often, it looked like they were just winging it.

Women do not have that luxury. You must prepare. When you make a suggestion or throw out an issue that needs discussion or negotiation, you'd better have the goods to back it up. If you face pushback, and you are not prepared then you risk building a negative reputation instead of a formidable one. Have the relevant issues, deal terms, talking points, research, precedents, and cases to support your position or argument.

Sometimes, people will interrupt you midsentence, saying things like, "I don't agree with you," or "You're not right." How do you handle that? Are you triggered? Take a look back at chapter 3 and all you learned about how you respond to triggers. A good approach is to take a breath, stay measured, and then respond. Maybe you go through the details of your position again? Or maybe you change your approach? Either way, follow your intuition and read the room. When I feel strongly about something or I am advocating a position for my client, it's all about convincing someone to get on my side. Preparation is key, and that's how I effectively communicate my points. But how I address it or where I address it is always situational. Remember, in business, we are in a patriarchal society, and you get more with honey than you do with vinegar. One thing to note, when people like you, they want to help you.

Sometimes if I am in middle of a stressful negotiation and tensions are high, I may start advocating some of my points with a bit of humor so that I am engaging and not perceived as a total bitch. That won't get you anywhere either.

Taking the time to prepare is essential. There aren't any shortcuts, because gender perception is still a real thing. Early on in my law practice, I learned to over-prepare, print my materials, distribute them at meetings, and when those in attendance are unprepared, sometimes we'd just continue with the meeting anyway. Sometimes we would actually reschedule the meeting. Either way, I thanked them for their time, even if it was a waste of mine.

I was lucky to learn from one of the best.

Afeni Shakur was a formidable force in the 1970s as a member of the Black Panther Party. As the section leader of the Harlem chapter, she helped with recruitment, ran the free breakfast program for children in the community, and actively helped tenants organize strikes against slumlords. However, on April 2, 1969, alongside other members, her activism led to her arrest in New York City. They were ultimately indicted on over 150 felony counts, having been set up on bogus charges by an FBI informant posing as a member of the Black Panther Party. They became known as The Panther 21.

Afeni and Joan Bird, the only other woman in the group, were sent to the Women's House of Detention in New York to await trial. After being presented with the leftover public defenders (the men in the party got the experienced ones), Afeni made a bold decision: she would represent herself. She thought: *If I'm going to be locked up for the rest of my life, the last voice anyone is going to hear is my own.* Needless to say, the male Panthers got wind of what she was doing and tried talking her out of it. When Afeni was released on bail, she stayed with her sister, Gloria Jean (Aunt Glo), in the Bronx and began preparing for the trial. She frequented the law library, pouring over legal books, and found inspiration in Fidel Castro's manifesto, *History Will Absolve Me.*

When the trial began in the fall of 1970, Afeni was commuting to court every day with Billy Garland, a Black Panther member from New Jersey who delivered the Panther Power newsletter around New York City. They had an intimate relationship, and in November 1970, while still representing herself in court, Afeni discovered she was pregnant.

On February 8, 1971, she learned that two other Panthers, who were now also out on bail, had fled.

As a result, the judge revoked her bail and remanded her back to the Women's House of Detention—now five months pregnant with Tupac. The first motion she filed with the court was for a daily glass of milk and an egg for her unborn child. Even in jail, Afeni continued to study and prepare her defense.

Her cross-examination of the confidential FBI informant was legendary. On April 28, 1971, seven months pregnant with Tupac, she delivered her closing statement and was ultimately acquitted of all charges in May. Tupac was born on June 16, and the rest is history. Preparation is key.

Learn the crucial art of self-advocacy, which is not the same as "tooting your own horn." If you *just happen* to get in the elevator at the same time as the boss, casually ask about attending that important invite-only industry event.

Also, give people enough rope to hang themselves. Most of the time, people who are unprepared and overconfident will make mistakes or lack the emotional intelligence to read the room. Overconfident people tend to talk too much, so let them. That's your chance to extract information you can use against them later if you need to. People always try to impress others with how much they know or how smart they think they are. "Always Say Less Than Necessary" is Law 4 in *The 48 Laws of Power* by Robert Greene.

I recommend that every woman in business read this book. While not everything will resonate or apply to your situation, it's definitely worth the read.

After Tupac died, one of his producers who had produced a lot of Tupac's music, including many of his unreleased tracks, found himself in a difficult position. Tupac never had a music lawyer, so when he passed away, many of his collaborators and songwriters sued the estate for unpaid royalties. No one— neither Tupac's estate nor the collaborators—was receiving any royalties because there were no formal agreements memorializing the deal points with the music creators.

It's important for music artists to have a music lawyer representing them, especially someone as big as Tupac. A music lawyer represents the artist in negotiations with record companies and music publishers to make sure the music artist gets a fair deal. Once an artist signs a record deal, their music lawyer handles all the paperwork, which includes drafting and negotiating the producer agreements and songwriter split agreements. These agreements are important because they clearly define who gets paid what.

Tupac didn't have any album agreements in place, which left everyone unpaid. This led to disputes over copyrights and royalties and was the reason why one of his producers sued Tupac's estate. In the music industry, artists often work on their songs with co-writers, and in the rap and hip-hop genre, one song can have multiple contributors. These include the song's producer, who usually brings the musical bed of the song or "the beat," other rappers, and anyone who writes and/or sings "the hook," which is the song's chorus.

Recordings or songs may also incorporate "samples"—snippets or replays of previously released hits. The songwriters of the sampled track are entitled to a percentage of the copyright in the new song. Anyone who uses a sample from an existing recording and/or song needs to get *written* permission from all relevant music creators and owners (i.e., artist, record label, songwriters, and music publishers) of the sampled song. This is mandated under the Copyright Law of the United States. See how complicated it all is? That's why having a music lawyer to handle the paperwork and the negotiations are essential.

So, there I was, working on the Tupac estate and helping Afeni get all the prior producer agreements and songwriter split agreements completed so everyone could receive their royalties, including Tupac's estate. The record company was holding all the money until the disputes were resolved and all the agreements were fully executed, which was a lot of work!

At the same time, Afeni had just won a major court case against Death Row Records, in which the court granted her ownership of all of Tupac's unreleased sound recording copyrights as his rightful beneficiary. This was a big win for her. Her next goal was to meet with this particular producer, the other rappers, and songwriters who also wanted to sue Tupac's estate so she could understand why they were upset and why their agreements weren't getting signed. She was genuinely confused over why her son's friends were upset. I knew why, but none of the lawyers wanted to hear what I thought. After all, I was a newbie intern lawyer.

I prepared my notes for the meeting, knowing it would be a heated discussion. The producer was particularly upset because all the lawyers argued that every songwriter, including him, should get equal splits for Tupac's songs. While this might look good on paper for the Tupac estate, it didn't reflect the reality of rap music. That's not what they did in the studio or on the street. No matter how many times I said it in the office, my boss didn't want to hear it. He just didn't get it, and he certainly didn't understand Black culture.

I created a separate list of all the disputed songs, detailing the splits based on actual contributions (i.e., the industry custom in rap music) rather than what copyright laws dictated. When we got to the meeting, chaos erupted almost immediately. The lawyers were fighting and arguing their points. The producer jumped up and screamed, "This is bullshit! I'm the producer, and I'm supposed to be getting 50 percent!"

I couldn't help myself. From my seat behind the table, I blurted out, "He's right." Suddenly, the room was in turmoil. My boss lost his shit and dragged me into the hallway, where he proceeded to chastise me for taking a position against our client, the Tupac estate. Afeni and Molly followed us out of the meeting. Afeni wanted to know what I was talking about.

I pulled out the copyright split sheet that I had prepared and explained how they divide up the song splits in rap and hip-hop music. My hands trembled as I handed it to her. Afeni, lighting up a Newport cigarette in the hallway of that big ass law firm in downtown Los Angeles, silently read over my notes before saying, "All right. We know what we need to do in there," and then she walked back into the room with my sheet in hand.

When I returned to my seat behind the table, Afeni turned to me and said, "No baby. You sit up here, right next to 'Feni." She made everyone shuffle down to make room for me to sit right next to her *at the table*. For the next two hours, we went through each song, discussing the copyright splits with all the music creators. The lawyers barely said another word.

That experience truly showed me how being over-prepared could save my ass; however, the reverse is also true. When you find yourself in a room where you don't feel as prepared as you should be, act as if you're prepared. Just be careful not to become over-confident and say too much. Talking too much can tip people off that you're not as prepared as you're pretending to be. Instead, focus on listening, learning, and taking notes. This way, by the next meeting, you'll be caught up and ready to kick ass. Becoming an expert takes time, and there will be times when you think you're prepared, only to realize you're not. It happens to everyone.

My over-preparedness hasn't only enabled me to fight for the rights and best deals for my clients but has empowered me to advocate for myself. It prevents me from being bullied or overlooked in meetings, whether at boardroom tables filled with men, or in discussions with high-ranking politicians. Preparation allows me to hold my position, keep my power, and steer discussions in the direction I want.

As a newbie in any field, it takes time to build confidence and expertise. However, never go into any meeting without preparing as thoroughly as possible. You owe it to yourself to be ready, and you won't do yourself any favors by appearing incompetent because you choose to wing it. In the end, preparation is not just a strategy—it's a necessity for success.

CHAPTER JOURNAL NOTES

- Seek all the resources that will help you get better at what you do. Books? Mentors? Classes?
- Ahead of your next meeting, challenge, or discussion, understand what knowledge you need to bring to the table before you walk into that room. Make a list. Do the research.
- Organize your talking points and have them handy. Customize them for the people you're meeting with, keeping in mind that they may not have the knowledge or understanding you do.
- Practice fine-tuning your point of view.
- What questions do you anticipate being asked about this subject? Know the answers.
- Cover all the bases—every possibility, not just the probabilities.
- If you find yourself unprepared, ask questions that elicit more information and focus on listening rather than talking.

9

Teach to Transform. Building Your Expert Status

When you teach something, you super-solidify information you already know and get better at articulating it. This is especially helpful for complicated subjects like copyright and royalty formulas and calculations for recording and publishing agreements.

Teaching others what you know is basically an advanced form of practice. The more you practice something, the better you get at it. Whether it's playing guitar, pickleball, or negotiating complex agreements, every time you practice, you become closer to achieving expert status. As a college student, I taught guitar lessons to kids, not only to earn extra money but to teach myself the songs I wanted my band to play. Before teaching a song to my students, I'd learn it and then practice it over and over. By the time I got to band practice, I practically knew the song by heart.

When I moved to Los Angeles and became an attorney, I applied the same strategy that had proven successful in learning and teaching guitar. Reading and trying to learn and draft all the deal points in the agreements felt overwhelming, especially since I didn't have a real music lawyer job and therefore had no practical experience. Newly sober and taking the music business class at USC with Don Passman, my brain felt like it was on fire! For fifteen weeks, I schlepped to downtown Los Angeles for that class, all for the sake of gaining experience.

One day at my internship, I met this big guy with long dreadlocks named Randy Ross, who worked in IT for lawyers and other entertainment companies during the day and played in his Rastafarian band at night. We hit it off immediately. One of his best friends, Kia Kamran, was a music lawyer working as a real lawyer in a real law firm—unlike me, who was interning for free. Randy connected me with Kia, and we began meeting regularly. Kia was a super cool guy. I told him about Don Passman's class, and he said he was working on a lot of the agreements I was learning about.

Kia offered me some templates—form copies of frequently used agreements that just need client information or negotiated deal terms filled in. Kia gave me a producer agreement and a songwriter split agreement, which was awesome. Meeting with Kia all the time helped me connect a lot of dots because I could talk through all the material.

At my internship, my boss had me organize his notes for upcoming revisions on a bunch of music law chapters in some specialized legal books, the *Matthew Bender Practice Guide* series. These weren't books you could buy at a bookstore; you had to subscribe to LexisNexis for an astronomical fee, and they'd send the revisions to you by mail. You'd then remove the old pages and insert the new ones—it was archaic as fuck! In those days, the internet had just become a *thing,* and while many of us had AOL accounts, law firms weren't really using the internet for anything other than sending emails, *sometimes.* The online world was still too big and scary, so a lot of lawyers refused to use it, instead relying on fax machines and postal services to send agreements across the country.

Working on my boss's notes and reading his updates on music business agreements for the Matthew Bender practice guide was invaluable for my learning journey. One day at work, my boss said he intended to stop editing the music law chapter revisions because they were too time-consuming. I begged him to let me help. He was ready to resign from the project, but since I was taking Don Passman's class and studying copyright law, I felt confident I could make a difference.

The boss had nothing to lose because he'd still have to approve everything I did as it was his name on the actual guides, not mine. I proposed gathering notes and chapter drafts from young, cool, practicing music lawyers who were working at real law firms that I now had connections to through all my networking. They could contribute and be credited for their little sections, but my boss would get credit for the whole thing. To my delight, he agreed to let me try. I was thrilled!

At the same time, I was working on some producer agreements for Jennifer Lopez's first album, *On the Six*, as my boss represented her. Things were really coming together for me. Finally! My new mission was to help the boss update his chapters in the Matthew Bender series. Little did I know, this would kick-start the next twenty-five years of my career in writing about trending music business topics. This eventually led to teaching the same type of class that Don Passman taught and editing the international music business legal books for the IAEL.

The following year, the Matthew Bender music law updated chapters were finally ready for publication. My boss even gave me a credit in his section.

By that time, I was working for him as a real lawyer, albeit earning only minimum wage. I learned so
much from helping him update those music business
chapters and discussing the issues with my new lawyer friends. That's what led to my decision to pursue
a part-time teaching job at the Musicians Institute in
Hollywood.

A lawyer I met while working on the Matthew
Bender chapter updates was Burgandy Morgan, and
she taught a copyright and music business class at
the Musician's Institute twice a week. It was she who
mentioned that they needed another teacher, so she
connected me with Kenny Kerner, the head of the
music business department. He took a liking to me
right away and hired me.

As my class grew, so did my skills as an attorney.
Teaching kept me current on all the laws and industry
customs. When I opened my firm in 2001, the music
business was evolving rapidly. People were starting to
consume music digitally instead of buying CDs, and
new methods for distributing and marketing music
were emerging daily.

I was eager to meet some of the big players in the
music business, but it seemed nearly impossible. I was
running a small law firm, not a prominent one with
big-name lawyers with big-name clients. Plus, I didn't
have famous parents to help me build connections.

So, I came up with a strategy: I invited some of the big guns to be guest speakers in my UCLA class. To my utter delight, they always accepted! After all, who doesn't love talking about themselves? This strategy helped me connect with some of the most successful people in the music industry who I wouldn't have had access to otherwise.

Since anyone could enroll in UCLA Extension classes, many students signed up to gain a competitive edge in the industry, including several practicing lawyers. Teaching that class became my way of grasping the material I needed to understand and the new deals and business points that emerged from the transition from physical to digital music distribution.

Inviting prominent figures in the music industry to speak to my students also presented opportunities to enrich my own knowledge. I could ask the questions I desperately needed answers to. While industry professionals understood their specific roles, they often lacked insight into other areas of the business. By bringing in experts from various sectors, I turned their "lectures" into massive tutorials for myself.

After these lectures, the students working in the music business would return to work and tell their colleagues and bosses about the guest speaker and what they learned. These students often returned to work

DINA LaPOLT | 201

armed with insights that surpassed what their bosses knew about certain issues.

As word spread over the years, more artists and songwriters were also taking my class. Bill Withers, who wrote "Lovely Day," "Just the Two of Us," "Lean on Me," "Ain't No Sunshine," and many other hits, sent his daughter to my class. Eddie Money's kids also took it, and so did some of the Chambers Brothers. It was a blast!

The atmosphere fostered curiosity and invited dialogue, allowing everyone to learn from these experts. This sense of community led to end-of-term dinners or hanging out because there was a sense of sadness each time the term came to an end.

My lectures resonated with most of the students because they were electrifying. Whether discussing publishing or touring, I made the topics interesting. Realizing the potential to share my insights, I decided to write articles about some of these hot-bed topics in the music business. I connected with a guy from Cosmik Debris, a monthly online music magazine, who'd attended the panel I took part in for the California Copyright Conference. He introduced himself and asked if I'd be interested in writing for the magazine, which marked my first foray into writing opinion pieces. Those articles quickly gained traction, and my students who read them sent them to their colleagues and friends.

As I continued to speak at various music industry conferences, I began writing articles for the panel attendees or getting them included in the conference materials. Eventually, I was asked to organize and moderate hot-topic panels, which led to becoming a keynote speaker at some events.

In 2011, when I was unanimously elected as the editor for *Building Your Artist's Brand as a Business* for the next MIDEM convention, I created a chapter outline to shape the book's structure. That was the first real project I did all on my own. I consulted with nearly 200 lawyers from all over the world who were part of the IAEL and asked some of them to contribute articles for the book. However, I created a bit of disruption because I was the first editor in IAEL history who had some seriously fucking high standards. I wouldn't accept just any submission. I insisted on contributors with genuine industry experience and a prominent reputation, whether in their home country or on whichever subject they wrote about.

Some of the pissed-off lawyers I'd rejected went to the chairman of the IAEL, Jeff Liebenson, complaining that they had been in the organization for thirty years and yet I had turned them down. They wanted him to intervene, but Jeff simply reminded them that I was the editor and had the authority to decide whose contributions made it into the book. He was literally my gatekeeper. And then when my book was published, it was an awesome achievement!

Since then, I've written countless op-eds and articles for *Billboard*, *Forbes*, *Variety*, and other leading publications on a wide range of issues and subjects. I tackled hot topics like the systemic racism of using rap and hip-hop lyrics against artists as evidence of in criminal cases, as well as the intricate copyright discussions during the passing of the *Music Modernization Act*. A lot of my colleagues joined me in this endeavor. It was exciting and fun to establish a standard where experts and professionals could share their knowledge.

In May 2017, after getting out of the California Rehabilitation Institute where I was recovering from my neck surgery, Congressman Doug Collins and I started talking regularly. Before the *Music Modernization Act* was introduced in Congress, Doug had sponsored a bill called the *Songwriter Equity Act*, which struggled to gain traction because it didn't get enough bipartisan support.

The *Music Modernization Act* emerged as a consolidation of three separate bills aimed at updating copyright law in response to the challenges posed by digital streaming and new technologies. After they had a real first outline of the MMA, Doug called me, asking, "What do you think songwriters need in this new iteration of the songwriter bill? Can you put a list together?"

I reached out to Michelle Lewis of SONA, and together we made a list. It highlighted the absence of songwriters at the negotiation table during legislative initiatives, the section of the *Copyright Act* that allowed record companies to collect and pay songwriter income, and a bunch of other issues that songwriters felt were unfair. Of course, the National Music Publishers' Association (**NMPA**) and the publishers were not happy. We advocated for including songwriters on the board of a new organization that would collect the mechanical royalty income from streaming platforms and pay the publishers and songwriters. Putting songwriters on the board of this new royalty collection entity was not something publishers wanted to do.

We also pushed for audit rights that would allow songwriters to directly audit this organization at no cost because traditionally only people with a lot of money can afford to conduct any audit. A lot of the publishers were pissed that I was telling Congressman Collins all of this, but he and his legislative director, Sally Rose Larson, were committed to establishing a direct line to songwriters instead of relying solely on the NMPA all the time. Doug recognized that the NMPA had no songwriters on its board, only music publishers.

The head of the NMPA, David Israelite, and its general counsel, Danielle Aguirre, were leading the charge on behalf of the music industry. While there were areas of agreement, there were areas where songwriters and publishers did not see eye to eye. Because of this, Doug and Sally Rose wanted to make sure they had direct relationships with the two largest songwriter advocacy groups: the Nashville Songwriters Association International (NSAI) and the Songwriters of North America (SONA).

When President Trump was elected in 2016, the Republicans held a majority in both the House and the Senate, so it was a great opportunity to get pro-copyright reform legislation passed. I thought, *I may as well get something good done while the entire country is going to shit for women, people of color, and the LGBTQ+ community.*

Doug made sure SONA was included in the legislative working group for the *Music Modernization Act*, which the publishers were leading. After years of meeting politicians and attending legislative hearings in Washington, D.C., the legislation passed in the House unanimously. However, it was a different story in the Senate. A major company that stood to lose a lot of money (because they'd have to pony up and finally pay songwriters what they deserved), had convinced a high-profile senator to try to kill the bill. On the very day of the Senate vote, September 18,

2018, we had to modify the final version of the bill to accommodate these fucking nutters!

In a frantic negotiation just two hours before the vote in the Senate cloakroom, Susan Genco led the charge on behalf of all our creator groups. It was an issue the record labels needed to support, but they sure as hell weren't going to listen to the music creator groups, the musicians' union, SAG-AFTRA (which they hated), or the music publishers, even though the three big publishers were owned by major record companies. The independent publishers are a formidable group that makes up a lot of the NMPA board.

Despite the record labels' reluctance to engage with music creators, Susan's deep relationships in the industry—having spent twenty years in legal and business affairs for the major record labels—helped bridge the gap, along with Mitch Glazier, head of the RIAA. On September 18, the bill passed in the Senate and was sent to President Trump, who would sign it into law the following month.

We were all set to fly to Washington, D.C. for the signing, but we were told to "scrub" our social media accounts of any partisan content before the White House compiled the invite list. Like many music creators, I'm a Democrat, and we all had partisan stuff on our social media accounts. So, we hired a third-party social media company, Crowd Surf, to scrub our accounts. A couple of weeks later, our names were submitted to attend the October 11 signing of the bill. However, the night before, while attending the Senate Judiciary celebration party in Washington D.C., I got an email disinviting me to the White House. Soon after, others at the party started getting the same email. The only one in our group still invited was Paul Williams, a major songwriter and chair of ASCAP, one of the largest performance rights companies in the United States.

The next day, on the flight back to Los Angeles, Beth Matthews, the CEO of ASCAP, stood up on the plane and turned around to the rest of us with her iPhone in hand and announced that Paul Williams had also just been disinvited—just hours before the event! We felt terrible for him because we were all on a flight back to Los Angeles and he was left there in D.C. So much for scrubbing our social media accounts! Watching President Trump sign the bill on C-SPAN, I couldn't help but notice that there was a sea of white guys in attendance, with only one woman and one Black man, the singer Sam Moore. It was a stark reminder of the work still needed in our country. Yikes!

CHAPTER JOURNAL NOTES

- Are you currently working in the field you're most passionate about?
- If so, who can you mentor or help get ahead by teaching them what you know.
- What are some of the things you can do to teach others? Make a list.
- If not, go re-read Chapter 5!

10

Give Back and
Help People

**Before I got sober in 1998, I really didn't
understand the concept of helping people, but
then I learned about *being of service*.** Nothing
helps you more than helping other people. Being of
service is a major theme of any recovery program.
Addicts are generally selfish and self-obsessed people,
but once they get sober, their focus shifts to being of
service to other people. Recovery literature specifically references an untreated alcoholic as an "egoma-
niac with an inferiority complex," a description that
could not be more truthful. News flash: Everyone
should do this because when you help others, it helps
you more!

Before I got sober, I only thought about myself and
how people could help me. Considering how I could
be of service to other people didn't come naturally

to me. Once I started helping people without expecting anything in return, it made a difference in my life. Starting in 1998, I learned about being of service and started applying the same concept professionally, especially after I became successful. This transformation was profound. The entertainment industry, especially in music, is a business of peaks and valleys. Some years you're up, but other years you're down. It's inevitable. In those tough times, your goal should be to have people lift you up rather than kick you.

Always be humble and ask others what *you* can do for *them*. I started giving back to my industry as a way of paying it forward because I recognized the many blessings in my life. I saw the impact I made on others in my UCLA class and volunteering with all the copyright reform legislation. This felt *great*! I realized that by staying positive and helping people, I could maintain high vibrational energy. A daily practice of recognizing all your blessings and paying it forward can go a long way . . . *for you!*

After I turned fifteen years sober, it looked like I finally had all the "bells and whistles." At least that's what it looked like on the outside but in reality I had hit an emotional wall and wondered, *is this all there is?* I had two beautiful boys and an amazing wife, my UCLA class was in high demand, I was speaking at music industry conferences all over the country, and

for all intents and purposes, my law firm was successful. But I was just feeling *blah*, and I didn't know why.

On Saturday mornings, I used to go to a recovery meeting in West Hollywood called "Survivors." It
was formed in the 1980s during the AIDS epidemic
and was a staple of my sobriety. A war veteran named
Dennis used to come to the meeting every week. When
he lost his home, he started living in the West Hollywood Park. Everyone loved him, even the West Hollywood law enforcement. We looked out for him by
bringing him food and coffee before meetings. From
time to time, people let him stay in their garages or
gifted him with a few nights at the La Cienega Motel.
Dennis always brought his guitar to meetings, so he
and I bonded over music. In recovery meetings, you
look for similarities rather than differences.

Over time, Dennis developed a neurological disorder, and his health deteriorated rapidly. Sometimes
he shook so badly, he couldn't walk and eventually
ended up in a wheelchair. People from the meetings
would pick him up and drive him to his doctors'
appointments at the veterans hospital. Despite the sei-
zures, he still came to the meeting every week with his
guitar strapped to the back of the wheelchair.

One Saturday morning, Dennis said he had a sei-
zure in the middle of the night and rolled over onto
his guitar, crushing it. He was devastated, and every-

one felt bad for him. The only thing he had that mattered anymore was that damned guitar.

That Monday, when I went to work, I just felt empty again. I started thinking about Dennis. Just then, I jumped up and told my assistant I had to run an errand. I got in my car and drove down to the park. I was literally running through the park like a crazy person, looking for Dennis. It was the dead of summer; I'll never forget it because I was sweating buckets. I finally found Dennis and told him, "Stay right there! I'm going to get my car. We have to go somewhere!"

I drove him to Guitar Center and had him pick out a guitar. I paid for the guitar, got him some food, and took him back to the park. He was literally crying. I told him how much I loved him and gave him a hug, and that fucking put me on a pink cloud. I was on top of the world after that. Dennis was so happy.

The next Saturday, Dennis was at the meeting with his new guitar. He'd named it Dina. He eventually passed away, but I felt like that act of service did more for me than it had for him. Since then, I've learned a new way to be of service. I started doing anonymous acts of kindness. I would do something for someone, expecting nothing in return, and the kicker was—I told no one what I did. This is a powerful intentional act that raises your vibration, and when you raise your vibration, you improve your mood and optimize your physical health.

Acts of kindness can be as simple as taking an elderly neighbor to the grocery store, dropping clothes or food items off at a homeless shelter, or paying for the person behind you in line at Starbucks. When your vibration is high, you attract others with the same vibrational levels. Certain thoughts and emotional patterns like peace, joy, love, forgiveness, and acts of service foster high-frequency vibrations compared to other mentalities like fear, sorrow, and resentment.

Philanthropy and volunteering for nonprofit organizations also help raise my vibration, keep my frequency high, and allow me to give back. In addition to SONA, I sit on multiple boards and/or executive leadership committees and this kind of work gives me a lot of personal gratification. Those organizations are all different from one another, and each allows me to be of service in a different way. I'm not just donating time and money or raising funds for them.

My efforts as an ally and activist in the Black community (thanks to my mother and Afeni Shakur) led me to serve on the executive leadership council of the Black Music Action Coalition (BMAC). I also co-author articles, comment papers, and sit on panels for BMAC with its chair and CEO, Willie "Prophet" Stiggers. BMAC was formed in 2020 to address the systemic racism within the music industry and to advocate on behalf of Black music creators and executives. In 2021, BMAC presented me with their Change Agent Award, alongside legendary civil rights attorney and activist, Ben Crump. Molly helped with the arrangements so BMAC could fly in Afeni's sister, Aunt Glo, from Atlanta to present it to me. They also created a tribute video which featured my mother. It was very special.

SONA and BMAC regularly team up on music creator advocacy initiatives, so there's a lot of synergy between the two organizations. The Recording Academy established the Entertainment Law Initiative (ELI) to encourage discussion and debate around legal affairs in the ever-evolving music industry and how they affect creators and the greater music community. By partnering with law schools nationwide, they offer year-round networking and career development events, cultivating the next generation through connections and educational opportunities for students.

The ELI Grammy Week Event, held the Friday before the Grammy Awards, connects music professionals and creators with industry leaders. It acknowledges music business trailblazers through the ELI Service Award, which is an accolade presented to a legal professional or entity who demonstrated commitment to advancing and bettering the music community through service. The annual ELI Writing Contest challenges law students to identify and research pressing legal issues that challenge today's music industry and outline a proposed solution in a 3,000-word essay. A nationwide panel of volunteer music law experts judge the papers in blind process to select a winner and two runners up, whose work is presented at the ELI Event.

Many of these law students went on to intern for prominent entertainment firms, and some became prominent entertainment lawyers themselves. In 2019, they honored me with the ELI Service Award, which Steven Tyler presented to me for my role in helping with copyright legislation and advocacy. It was a day I'll never forget. Now, I give back by serving on their executive committee.

I'm also on the Music, Film, and Entertainment Industries board of City of Hope, where I help raise money to support cancer research. City of Hope is one of the largest and most advanced cancer research and treatment organizations in the United States and a leading research center for diabetes and other life-threatening illnesses. Every October, we host the Spirit of Life Gala, our annual fundraising campaign, where we recognize and honor a leader for their exceptional contributions to their community and profession. Through my influence at City of Hope, I have been able to assist people in the music industry with cancer by connecting them with the right people in the organization who guide them through the health insurance red tape and get them in for further tests.

Given the importance of my sobriety and recovery, I help and/or serve on two boards that provide support and resources to people struggling with substance abuse disorders. The first is Friendly House, which was founded in 1951. It's the oldest residential program in the United States dedicated to helping women recovering from drug and alcohol abuse. I was on their board after receiving the Visionary Award at their Annual Awards Luncheon in 2022, alongside my buddy, Paul Williams, who was honored as Person of the Year and is also a longtime member of the sober recovery community.

Friendly House's mission is to inspire and empower women of all gender experiences on their journey to overcome substance abuse disorders and mental health challenges. They offer detox and residential facilities, and a sober-living residence where women can slowly transition after rehab back into the community, often with their children. Although I am no longer on the board, I am still very involved with the organization.

I joined the Neil Lasher Music Fund board in 2022, established in memory of Neil Lasher, a prominent music executive who passed away in 2020 due to complications from coronavirus. He'd been thirty-eight years sober when he died. Neil was known for being of service to those in the music business struggling with addiction. He would drop everything to help an alcoholic or addict in need. Neil's life partner, Jill Jordan, started the fund, which is administered by the Caron Foundation and provides grants for people in the music industry and their families.

I serve on this board to make sure people in my industry struggling with addiction can access a reputable rehabilitation program. The recovery industry, like so many others, has its share of crooks and scammers who set up sham drug and alcohol "rehab" and "sober living" facilities that do nothing more than steal your money. It's a real shame, especially when the people who love and support addicts try to get them into rehab but have no idea where to go or how the system works. Too often, friends and family members just search for drug and alcohol rehab programs online. This poses a serious danger, potentially leading to their placement in an untrustworthy facility. In my experience and the experience of millions and millions of other sober people, any facility or rehab program that does not incorporate the 12 steps of Alcoholics Anonymous is not reputable.

With the Neil Lasher Music Fund, we provide funding and have an exclusive relationship with the Caron Foundation, one of the most prominent and reputable rehabilitation centers in the United States. It was founded over seventy years ago by Richard and Catherine Caron in Wernersville, Pennsylvania. With two inpatient facilities, four outpatient locations, and a recovery center, Caron has helped thousands of people struggling with substance abuse disorder. They are licensed and accredited by the Commission on Accreditation of Rehabilitation Facilities and adhere to the highest levels of practice standards. Like Caron, many reputable and licensed rehabilitation facilities accept various insurance plans, making quality care accessible to those in need.

To help others, I need to be emotionally, mentally, and physically stable. If I can't hold it together for myself, I can't do it for other people. Giving back helps me get out of my own head. I once heard in a meeting, "My mind is a bad neighborhood, and I don't go there alone." We all face stressors, and when I feel depressed, deflated, angry, or overwhelmed, I take a moment and ask myself, "What's right in my life?"

I've conditioned myself to pause and write a quick gratitude list on a Post-it note, my iPhone, or even a napkin. Sometimes, I snap a photo of my surroundings and share it on my Instagram story as a *gratitude list*. These photos might capture a beautiful sunny day, a warm breeze across my face, the kind Starbucks barista, or my boys' laughter. When I find myself caught up in thoughts beyond my control, a simple gratitude list or a post can quickly pull me out of my own head.

CHAPTER JOURNAL NOTES

- To what organizations would you be willing to volunteer your time?
- What strengths do you have that can contribute to some of these organizations?
- What could you do to get involved in your community?
- What are you grateful for?
- How are you contributing to someone else's well-being?

Conclusion

Becoming successful in a high-stress, male-dominated, competitive environment is entirely possible. You don't need to attend an Ivy League school or come from a wealthy family. For most people, success didn't come naturally. It didn't just fall into their lap—it came from good old fashioned hard work.

Compared to my colleagues and peers, I was at a significant disadvantage. I was a musician battling addiction, grappling with emotional triggers, and often plagued by self-doubt that would thwart my confidence. Growing up in a patriarchal society, I didn't have many role models, and then I pursued a male-dominated career. I learned to accept my circumstances and focus on my goals.

Accept where you are in life and then consider what you want and where you want to be. Believe in yourself, even if you don't have support right now.

You have to put yourself first and make yourself a priority. Get to know your triggers so you can control your reactions before they can control you.

Emotions can become overwhelming, and they can easily throw you off track. One strength of becoming *street smart* is trusting your intuition and developing your emotional intelligence. In many ways, your emotional quotient (EQ) is more important than your intelligence quotient (IQ). It will help you survive and win battles. Take time to deep-dive into your soul and really get to know yourself; understand your strengths and weaknesses. Commit to capitalizing on what works while addressing what doesn't. Start with small, actionable steps toward your goals.

Action moves us forward—a continuum of thoughts, plans, and hopes is not enough. You have to move. Make each step manageable and realistic. Adjustments are part of the journey, but stay focused on taking action. *Remember, nothing changes if nothing changes.*

Build your skill set and lay a solid foundation for your future. This takes a lot of hard work and determination. Do it by any means necessary. Pursue education, seek mentorship, gain experience through internships and volunteer work, and be willing to start at the bottom. Don't think anything is beneath you. Consider becoming an assistant to someone you want to be like. Education is important, but you also need the experience to build a solid foundation.

The bottom is most often where we learn the most important lessons. Take everything in—every mistake, every wrong turn, and every failure, and learn from it. This is how you build experience. It doesn't come from success alone.

Preparation is essential. Present yourself confidently and read the room or feel the situation. You can still look like a million bucks even when you're not making boatloads of money (yet!). This gives you strength and confidence. People can sense it the instant you walk into a room. When you're prepared, you know your business inside and out. Know every angle and possible outcome before you walk into a negotiation. Your success hinges on your knowledge. When you're prepared, opportunities present themselves.

Advocacy and negotiation skills can be fine-tuned over time. It's just as important to understand who you want to be as who you don't. No one will advocate for you as effectively as you can. As you grow more knowledgeable, share your insights with others— you'll see and hear differing opinions and thoughts that enhance your own knowledge. And whenever you can, find ways to give back. Be selfless. Helping others fills you with love, joy, and forgiveness, which increases your vibration frequency. You have the choice to be more positive. And when you're down, the best way to raise your spirits and feel connected again is by doing good for others. My journey was a difficult one, but I put in the work. I never gave up. If you put in the hard work, you will be successful, too.

Become street-smart. Become a powerhouse, or a power woman. Commit to your dreams. Chart your path to your goals. Take that first step and never look back!

Acknowledgments

I want to thank everyone who impacted my journey, especially my mother, Donna Rae LaPolt. You were the queen of reinventing yourself and . . . I am my *mother's daughter.* Mom, one day I will see you on the other side of the Rainbow Bridge!

My twin boys, Wilson Ray and Buddy Lee . . . everything I do is for you.

My ex-wife, Wendy Goodman . . . you were one of the best things that ever happened to me.

Our savior and *de facto* family member, Angela Haro . . . thank you for always being there.

My brother Glenn and my sister Corinne . . . thank you for always having my back, being my foundation, making me laugh, and keeping me grounded.

My amazing sister-in-law, Melissa "Mel" LaPolt.

My nieces and nephews, Josie, Brian, Tessa, Ella, Rio, and Rexie . . . don't ever be afraid to take risks.

Michael "Jay" Goodman, Susan "VV" Brodner, Sarah and Rick, Mowie and Gramps.

The beginning . . .

My father, Robert LaPolt, Aunt Nancy (a.k.a. "chairman of the board"), Aunt Patty, Aunt Roxy (RIP), Uncle Renno, and all my cousins.

My music teachers, Mrs. Bythemia Bagley and John Anderson (RIP), Pattie Steffens and Lynne Davis (RIP), and New Paltz, N.Y.—what a gift it was to be raised there.

Jill Stevens . . . forever and a day. The late Eric Carr from KISS, Jedi Productions, SUNY New Paltz, and Gail Parisi for getting me in. Professors Steve Ford, Mary Jane Corry, Lee Pritchard and Dr. Nancy Kassop.

Joan Jett, Kenny Laguna, Elliot Saltzman, and my queen Carianne Laguna Brinkman—here we are almost forty years later!!!!

Chana Hall, Doug Steele, and of course Ted Christie for changing my life and driving with me to Cali in my 1987 yellow Ford Mustang. Brian Maguire, John Klepeis, Nicole A, Enterprise Rent-A-Car.

Aunt Peggy and Uncle Bob . . . You had me at my worst and saw me at my best.

My John F. Kennedy School of Law crew, Former Dean Ken Meade, Professor Dan Russo, Carrie Bozeman (RIP), Litta Pettus, Phyllis Beech, Kathy Gardiner, and Elsa Ortiz.

Sarah Kates, and San Francisco, music lawyers Deena Zacharin and Tony Berman.

My Irresistible Impulse music family . . . Ron Burris, Karen Whitham, Linda Snowden, Michelle "Snacker" Patterson, Stacy Arnett, Karen "Chew It" Smith, Jeanessa Morrison, Marissa Bernetti, and JR's Night Club. Eddy "Failure Is Not an Option" Augustin.

Carrie "Miss June" Stevens . . . thank you. I love you more than you will ever know. Hugh Hefner (RIP), Richard Bann, Mary O'Connor, the Playboy Playmates (you know who you are!), Anthony Benson, and the Conga Room. Michael Holdaway, my Eskimo!—here we are twenty-seven years later, from the Playboy Mansion to the rooms of recovery . . . you saved my life.

Robert Taylor (RIP), Liga, Stacy, Candida, Pony, and the Log Cabin and the West Hollywood recovery community. Wendy Slavkin, Sable, and my amazing sponsor Jane Stavish-Ryan and her wife, the legend herself, Lila Ryan . . . you are my surrogate parents. My sobriety sister and brother, Ginger Geary and Chaz Bono, all the European Countesses, and of course my favorite sober clairsentient, Karuana Gatimu—THANK YOU.

The middle . . .

The late, great Afeni Shakur for believing in me, even when I didn't believe in myself.

The greatest rap artist and poet-activist who ever lived, Tupac Shakur.

My ride-or-die and sister for life, Molly Monjauze.

Little Carl, Gloria "Aunt Glo" Cox, Jamala, Dr. Scottie, Billy and Kenny Lesane, Imani Lesane, Staci Robinson, Jamal Joseph, Preston Holmes, Karolyn Ali (RIP), Vatana Shaw, Claudio Cueni, Lauren Lazin, The Outlawz, Tom Whalley, Jimmy Iovine, Liza Joseph, David Cohen, Darryl Franklin, Dennis Dennehy, Jeff Harleston, Marnie Nieves, Erica Savage, Tanya Greig-Perara, Lisa Rogell, Tom Sturges, Sandy Fox, Kia Kameron, Wofford Denius,

Gary Fine, Kris Munoz, Damian Elahi, Brigitte Hales, Miles Copeland, Stevo Glendinning, Ed McMahon and Next Big Star, Stefanie Ridel, Renee Sandstrom, Stacey "Fergie" Ferguson, Ron Fair, John Duran, Joel Loquvam, Joe Mani, Burgandy Morgan and the Musician's Institute, Pascale Cohen-Olivier and UCLA Extension, Mick Mars, Tommy Lee and deadmau5, Mighty Mike Murga, Dean Wilson, Allen Kovac, Lewis Kovac, Chris Nilsson, Doug Mark, Barbara Berkowitz, Pam Malek, Howard Bragman (RIP), Val Allen, my legal warrior badass Christine Lepera, Don Passman, Jay Cooper, Joel Katz, Irving Azoff, Jeffrey Azoff, Jeff Liebenson and the International Association of Entertainment Lawyers (IAEL), Jack Struble, the one-and-only Steven Tyler, Mia Tyler, Chelsea and Taj, Aimee Preston, Joe and Billie Perry, Howard Kaufman (RIP), Caroline Kaufman, Rob Stringer, Jeff Smith, Kelly Bush, Lizzie Hardy, Simon Fuller, Jeff Frasco, Mick Fleetwood, Carl Stubner, Baby Bash, Paula DeAnda, Fifth Harmony, Josh Kelly, Andy Biersack and Black Veil Brides, Blasko, Offset, and Josh Edmund.

A very special thanks to Rosemary Caroll and Jill Berliner, the two power women/music lawyers who inspired me while I was in law school!

To all my power women badasses who continue to inspire and lift me up, Lou Taylor . . . you are beautiful inside and out. Mary J. Blige, Latonya Blige, Ashley Acevado, Cardi B, Patientce Foster, Jody Gerson, Renee Karalian, Laurie Soriano, Sylvia Rhone, Julie Greenwald, Michelle Jubelirer, Allison Statter, Lisa Moore, Shay Lawson, Carianne Marshall, Lisa Bonner, Shawn

Holley, Stacy Fass, Irene Lee, Christine Shin, Lila Gerson, Cheryl Paglierani, Celine Joshua, Julie Swidler, Stephanie Yu, Erica Bellarosa, Rani Hancock, Jeanette Perez, Lanre Gaba, Rayna Bass, Karen Kwak, Claudia Butsky, Laura Swanson and Gina Harrell, Yasmine Pearl, Lindsay Wagner, Dana Lowy, Gelareh "G" Rouzbehani, Jenny Swiatowy, Haley Reinhart, Sophie Hintze, Morgan Wade, Mary Sparr, Katie Clark, Nancy and Jennifer Zimmerman, Abby Anderson, Andile Ndluvo, Kendra Scott, Nancy Jacobsen, Debra Delshad, Tinashe, Simonne Solitro, Michaela Jae Rodriguez, Kaily Nash, Amanda Moore, Beata Murphy, Lisa Worden, Heather Lowery, Golnar Khosrowshahi, Rebecca Warfield, Tara Beikae, and Shannon Bayersdorfer.

Eddie Money (RIP) . . . I miss and love you. Thank you for all the lessons you didn't even know you were teaching me! Laurie Money and Jesse Money—never forget who you are.

She'yaa Bin Abraham-Joseph "21 Savage," Heather Joseph, Justin "Meezy" Williams, Booshie, the brilliant and incredible Sally Velazquez, and Chuck Kuck. Thank you for coming into my life. It's an honor and a privilege.

My perpetual co-counsel, whether he likes it or not, Larry Rudolph, and the power women at 724 Management, Jesse Peters, Tessa Bird, and the one-and-only Shabs Mohammed.

My Timeline Queens Alexis Fisher (my diva warrior), Susie Dunner, Lizzie Saunders, Anastasia "Stas" Karanikolaou, and, of course, Jamie Lynn Spears . . . you taught me how to be a better mom. David Weise, Steven Macauley, Laurie Davis and the late Beth Sabbagh . . . I miss you, my friend.

Steve Longo for *literally* saving my life in 2017. Dr. Ariella Morrow, Dr. Terrance Kim, and the California Rehabilitation Center. Julie Pilat, Lori Rischer, Dan Dymtrow, Talia, Mika Guillory, and the Friday Morning Hike Club crew for helping me walk again.

SoulCycle, Angela Manuel Davis, Veronica Everett, Tatiana Hachett, King Drew High School, and the entire Urban Fitness 911 crew!

My scrappies, sisters in advocacy, lifelong warriors and SONA co-founders, Michelle Lewis and Kay Hanley . . . I love you, my ride or dies! Erin McAnally, Kellie Brown, and all the SONA Warriors, including the early OGs Jack Kugell, Shelly Peiken, Adam Gorgoni, Adam Dorn, Pam Sheyne, Brendan Okrent, Gerry Fox, and our bestie, Liz Naftaly.

My warrior homies Susan Genco, Jordon Bromley and the Music Artists Coalition, my brother from another mother, Willie "Prophet" Stiggers, Caron Veazy, and the Black Music Action Coalition, and the late Jay Rosenthal. . . thank you for being my policy mentor. I love and miss you, my friend.

Power lobbyist and music publisher warrior, David Israelite and the small but mighty, amazing lawyer (and overall badass) Danielle Aguirre, Jacqueline Charlesworth, Evan Bogart, Ross Golan, Ann Chaitovitz, Shira Perlmutter, Cary Sherman, Beth Matthews, Lauren Iossa, Barbara Cane, Barbie Quinn, Ann Sweeny, Mitch Glazier, Michele Ballantyne, Daryl Freidman, Harvey

Mason Jr., Jeff Bennett, and Duncan Crabtree-Ireland, Kevin Liles, and Phil Wolosky. Congressmembers Hank Johnson, Jerry Nadler, Maxine Waters, Judy Chu, Zoe Lofgren, Debbie Wasserman-Schulz, and Linda Sanchez. Former congressman Doug Collins and Sally Rose Larson. Former congressmember and Los Angeles Mayor, Karen Bass.

The one-and-only Shirley Halperin, Lynne Segall, my love Dennis Lavinthal, Melinda Newman, Hannah Karp, Gail Mitchell, Thom Duffy, and Jem Aswad.

Jill Jordan, Todd Whitmer, Paul Willliams, Harold Owens, Bill Touteberg, Greg Sowders, Michael McDonald and the Neil Lasher Music Fund, Ebone Smith and We Are Rise. Christina Simos, Morgan Mallory and the Friendly House. Evan Lamberg and the president of our Music, Film, and Entertainment Industry Board at City of Hope, the amazing Alissa Pollack.

My bestie, Maria Arellano (whose candle will never have to stand alone), Sonia Rojo for giving me the opportunity to evolve, and Cynthia Costas Cohen for showing me that was the Universe's purpose.

AND FINALLY . . . last, but definitely not least . . .
My partners, attorneys, and all of you at LaPolt Law—THANK YOU for being my family, and let's keep building! You are all incredible, Lindsay Arrington-Chaklos, Dominic Chaklos, Kristin Wenning, Tom "The Dean" Dean, Mariah Comer, Cierra Carter, Mariana Alves-Ament, Daniela Jones, Manon Peri, Corey Bell, Anoop Sidhu, Stacy Holland, Randy Ross, Noah Ross, Rochelle

Ross, Wayde Westling, Craig Dahlerbruch, Marissa Botticelli, and Cherie DiSalvo. In addition, thank you to Paige Rauch (RIP), Sabrina Ment, Heidy Vaquerano, Jessie Winkler, Danielle "Deyonce" Price-Saunders, Andrew Bozeman, Vanessa Siravo, Steve Gagliano, John Meller, Josh Love, Cameron Berkowitz, Sarah Scott, Wylie Heiner, Rebecca Reynolds, Ellen Ahern, Keli Tomack, and Denise Coletta at CNB for being an important part of my journey.

My wellness and beauty team, which includes the fabulous Jana-Lee "Barbie" Cecchi, Melina Farhadi, Angel Dobbins, David Hamblin, and Farron Fowler, my personal trainer and makeshift dating coach! Shani Darden and her team of fabulous-nesses, including Emily Montague-Dayoub, DhananJaya "DJ" Nieto, Christine Son and The Things We Do, Dr. Rob Huizenga, Dr. Nader Yermian, Dr. Nadini Verma, Dr. Marc Makhani, Dr. David Alessi, and Dr. Kevin Kevorkian.

The next chapter . . .

My LaPolt Media, Street Smart and Stiletto Room crew—Sanjay Burman, Barbara Adhiya, Lara Hendrickson, Ashton Price, and everyone at Burman Books Media. Chirag Sarag, and the Mission Matters guys.

My director Mike Melendy for making me look like a million bucks! Legendary songwriter and vocalist Siedah Garrett (and her fabulous husband and manager Erik Nuri), Johannes Joergensen and Lars Halvor Jensen from DeeKay Productions for co-writing and producing *The Stiletto Room* theme song!!!

Dawn Kamerling, Crystal Henderson, and Brian Braiker, from the Press House. Cassie Petrey, Summer Rodriquez, Brooke Kier, and Natalie Sanden from Crowd Surf, and the amazingly brilliant Samantha Gayle Bullock for rounding up all of us feral cats! *I love you, my friend. Let's go!* This is just *another* beginning!

www.ingramcontent.com/pod-product-compliance
Ingram Content Group UK Ltd.
Pitfield, Milton Keynes, MK11 3LW, UK
UKHW021859080925
462717UK00017B/119

9 781722 599102